DROP
the
DEBT
WEIGHT

DROP
the
DEBT
WEIGHT

7 STEPS TO TAKE YOUR LIFE BACK!

KEMBALA EVANS

KPE

KP Evans Financial

Drop the Debt Weight
7 Steps to Take Your Life Back!

This book is intended to provide accurate information on the subject matter covered. However, it is sold with the understanding that the publisher and author are not engaged in rendering legal, accounting or other professional services. If legal or other expert assistance is required, the services of a competent professional should be sought. The author and publisher specifically disclaim any loss, liability, or risk as a result of application or use of any of the contents in this book.

This book may provide links to other websites and the publisher and author provide no warranty for other sites. Sites that may be linked have their own policies. Users may reference their terms of use and privacy policy prior to any use. Furthermore, the publisher and author do not endorse, approve or accept any liability for these types of other websites. Any use you make of the content linked to websites, is at your own risk.

Published by KP Evans Financial
info@gainmoneycontrol.com; http://gainmoneycontrol.com.

Author Photo: Doug Birkenheuer; BirkenheuerPhotography.com
Book Interior Design: Adina Cucicov

ISBN: 978-0-9835796-0-1

First Edition

DEDICATION

Debt is a four-letter word that can feel like a heavy weight on your shoulders. The financial pressure can be enormous. If you are burdened with debt, you are not alone. There are millions and millions of Americans struggling with debt every day.

This book is dedicated to anyone who is sick and tired of being in debt. To those who want to drop the debt weight, so they can truly take their lives back.

ACKNOWLEDGEMENTS

THIS BOOK STARTED as a dream. The kind you wake up to and still remember vividly afterward. My dream was so inspiring, that I thought to myself, I have to write a book to help people get out of debt. Too many people are struggling with debt. And this is negatively impacting people's lives.

Financial stress can make people feel hopeless and anxious. Worst of all, money problems could lead to health problems, murder-suicides, domestic violence, and divorces. Sadly, many people feel they have to portray an "everything is fine" image on the outside. They think no one cares about their issues anyway. It is this feeling of loneliness that often compounds the problem.

Well, I care about people struggling with debt. I am full of gratitude for the vision and fortitude to write this book to help you get rid of debt. As with many things in my life, I have not done this alone.

I appreciate those who have contributed:

- To my husband Sam for always believing in me. I appreciate your genuine perspective and unwavering support in everything. You are a real blessing!

- To my daughters, Aaliyah and Kiara, for lasting encouragement, having a listening ear, and sharing insightful thoughts and opinions. You inspire me!

- To my mother Susan, who helped shape me into the person I am today. Thanks for always being in my corner and offering your sage wisdom in life!

- To my father Bevin for planting the important seeds of gaining knowledge and being persistent into my life. I appreciate the time you spent reading this manuscript and offering excellent suggestions.

- To my dear Uncle Gres for everything you've ever taught me about life and money. You are a true gem!

- To my brother Keino, sister Anika, and Aunt Patricia for great insights and thoughtful feedback.

- To my dear friends, especially:

  - Valerie Henry and Anita Ibe for taking the time to read this manuscript. I appreciate your feedback and honest opinions on this work!

  - Lanee Blaise, Alphonso Brown, Lisa Bullard, Carmelita Crenshaw, Monty Cyriac, Joy Lee, Mary Mrowicki, Elba Pena, Jamillah Washington, Stephanie Williams, and Teresa Williams for constant support, interest, and helpful feedback.

- Kai Holmes for time spent reading this book to provide editorial help and useful suggestions.

- To my family and friends for invaluable feedback, helpful support, and sharing your personal experiences.

- Lastly, I would like to give a special shout out to the people who have contributed your valuable input, thoughts, and opinions on debt to this book. While I have not yet had the pleasure of meeting all of you—thank you for sharing your perspectives!

TABLE OF CONTENTS

Introduction 1

Step 1: Don't Beat Yourself Up About Past Mistakes 13

Step 2: Mind Over Debt 19

Step 3: Set Your Goals 27

Step 4: Create Your Debt-free Action Plan 33

Step 5: Pay Down Debt Faster 43

Step 6: Watch Your Debt 53

Step 7: Celebrate Your Successes! (WaaaHoo!) 57

Stay Focused on Your End Goal 59

Real Talk on Student Loans 65

    Why Student Loan Debt Matters 67

    Student Loan Debt Can Be Crippling 69

    What You Need to Know about Student Loan Debt 73

    How to Minimize Student Loan Debt 75

How to Pay Off Student Loan Debt.................................86

What if You Can't Afford the Payments?.........................88

Biggest Student Loan Mistakes to Avoid.........................90

Student Loan Debt in America—Survey Says...................100

Debt Settlement...109

Read This Before You Settle Any Debt...........................109

What You Need to Know about Debt Settlement Companies....110

Know Your Rights and Stop Debt Collector Abuse.........117

Are You Being Sued for Your Debt?...............................121

Has a Debt Collector Violated Your Rights?....................122

Who is Responsible for a Loved One's Debt after Death?....122

INTRODUCTION

"You wanna fly, you got to give up the
thing that weighs you down."
—Toni Morrison

DEBT IS TRICKY. It feels good when you're approved for a mortgage on a new home, or when student loans open the door to a college education. And you can't beat the convenience, perks, and purchasing power of credit cards. That's all good stuff!

When you manage debt effectively, you can enjoy the benefits more freely. For example, people who pay their credit card in full every month don't have to worry about paying high-interest rates on purchases or extra fees. They can just sit back, relax, and appreciate the perks like cash back, frequent flyer miles, and reward points.

On the flip side, too much debt can feel like a heavy weight on your shoulders. It's not just the thought of owing money that's the burden, but also the debt collector calls, bad credit reports, repossessions, liens, and foreclosures that could follow. Too much debt can be stressful, depressing, and downright embarrassing.

What's the best solution for burdensome debt? To pay it off and get rid of it—so you can take your life back.

You may be thinking, *it's easier said than done.* And that's often the case. As Henry Wheeler Shaw once said, "Debt is like any other trap, easy enough to get into, but hard enough to get out of."

The good news is that you can get out of debt. That's right: You can get out of debt!

Don't like being in debt? Get rid of it. YOU can make it happen! And this book will help you do just that.

Before we get started, I want you to take a moment and think about how you'll feel when you get rid of debt—for good! No more throwing money down the drain, high-interest payments, annoying debt collector calls, or sleepless nights.

Imagine yourself totally debt-free! Yes, *completely debt-free.* I want you to take a few minutes to THINK about how different your life would be without any debt. No more payments on anything, you own everything!

Let the thought of being debt-free really sink in. How different would your life be without any debt? How would you feel?

Go ahead take a deep breath, close your eyes, relax, and just imagine yourself debt-free...

Now ask yourself: Is everything you just imagined being debt-free worth it?

Of course it is. Be committed to becoming debt-free and make it a reality.

"If it's to be, it's up to me!"

Have you ever heard the saying "If it's to be, it's up to me"? In other words, it starts and ends with YOU. That means *you'll have to be the one to get you where you want to be.* You are in the driver's seat and in complete control of achieving your goals in life.

Yes, you're in complete control. Nothing happens until you do something. When you take the first step and keep marching towards your goal, you're bound to get there.

In my experience, I've learned that real change comes from the inside out. After all, *to accomplish anything in life, you must have the desire to do so inside.* The real secret to your success comes from within.

This holds true for whatever you want to achieve in life. You have to make the decision first. It doesn't matter what I think—or what anyone else thinks, for that matter. It has to be your decision. In the end, *you will only do what you want to do.* And you must do to make anything happen.

"Only I can change my life.
No one can do it for me."
—Carol Burnett

That being said (or should I say written), are you ready to drop the debt weight? I sure hope so, because I'm going to show you how to do it step-by-step. The techniques in this book will help you *give your debt the smackdown* it deserves.

DEBT IS MODERN-DAY SLAVERY

"Debt is the slavery of the free."
—Publilius Syrus

Are you working every day to pay Visa, MasterCard, Discover, your car note, or any other creditor? If your paycheck gets sucked up paying everyone else but yourself, then yes, *you're a slave to your lenders.*

It may be a tough pill to swallow right now, but it's the truth. And you must be willing to face the truth to change it. Just like an alcoholic has to admit he or she has a problem to get help. To fix any problem, you have to see it as one first.

Given that you're reading this book, you already know that. In fact, there are many people *who know they need to get out of debt.* That's why it's always a popular New Year's resolution every year. Sadly, fewer than 10 percent succeed at doing it.

Why are 90% of these people failing to get out of debt?

Could it be they don't know how to eliminate debt? Where to start? Or what to do?

Most people want to know how to get out of debt. They ask me:

- How do I get out of debt?
- Should I go through one of those debt consolidation companies?
- What do you think about claiming bankruptcy?
- Should I take out a loan against my 401K to pay off my credit cards?
- What about using a home equity line of credit to pay it down?
- And the list goes on and on.

I understand why they ask. It gets confusing, especially with all of those ads for so-called debt solutions out there. Often, those "so-called solutions" just get your hopes up and leave you with empty promises. Even worse, they could put you further in debt.

Still, they prey on our hopes—and make getting out of debt sound super easy to do. But it's not. A good rule of thumb to follow is: **if it sounds too good to be true, it probably is.** Or as Chester the Banker once told me, **"If it sounds too good to be true, it ain't!"**

The truth is, there is no silver bullet or quick fix for debt unless you happen to come into a windfall of cash. Or if you're lucky enough to have a generous person pay off your debt. That's what happened when Billionaire Robert Smith paid off all of the student loan debt (students, parents, and guardians included) for the 2019 Morehouse College graduating class. Could you imagine being one of those students with student loan debt hearing that announcement? While it's unbelievable to see $35,000—$40,000 in debt wiped out like that, the chances of this happening to the rest of us are slim to none.

There's still good news anyway.

In this book, you'll discover how to tackle your debt yourself without winning the lottery. You will learn how to use proven debt payment strategies to pay it off for less. It will also help you overcome the stumbling blocks to achieve success. That way, you're not a slave to your debt anymore!

WHAT DOES DEBT MEAN TO YOU?

"Debt is the worst poverty."
—*Thomas Fuller*

Sometimes kids say the most insightful things. My daughters have always shown a great interest in what I do. They probably know more about personal finance than many of the kids their ages after watching me and reading financial books.

At the time I began this writing, my then six-year-old asked me, "Mommy, what are you writing this book about?"

"Debt. Do you know what debt is?" I responded.

"Yes. Debt is something that hurts you," my daughter replied.

I looked at her and smiled. "Yes, that's an interesting way to look at it."

Then she went on and explained, "It's like when people go on a diet because something is really hurting them."

Wow! I raised my hand and gave her a big high five. I said, "Yes, that's a great definition of debt."

I was completely amazed that she understood the negative impact too much debt can have on someone's life. I loved her comparison. You see either way you look at it, carrying too much weight or too much debt could lead to health problems.

Did you know money problems are the #1 cause of stress? And stress kills.

Medically speaking, stress causes health problems like heart attacks and strokes. So my daughter's right—debt can hurt you. That's another reason to drop the debt weight—so you can feel better and live healthier.

Given her definition, I decided to ask my friends what they thought about debt. I asked, "When you think of debt, what comes to mind?" And their responses came rolling in:

"For me, when I think of debt, I see shackles and chains. It really destroys your sense of freedom. I knew of a young lady who felt both trapped and without hope due to her student loan debt. Very, very sad."

"Bondage to the point of modern-day slavery. Breaking bricks along the highway of a life most people never intended."

"Different forms of debt give me different feelings. I don't like having a mortgage, but I don't feel the same guilt that I would with retail or car debt. For me, the one thing I remember was embarrassment when bringing new items into the house."

"There is good debt and bad debt. Lots of people can't tell them apart, however."

"Lots of bills with no ability to save money."

"Overwhelming, stuck, how do I escape?"

"Education loans . . . ughhhh."

"Loss of opportunity, self-confidence, self-worth, and control."

"Lack of control, inability to make the best choices."

Can you relate to what they are saying about debt? These are mostly negative thoughts, feelings, and comments.

> *"There is scarcely anything that*
> *drags a person down like debt."*
> —P. T. Barnum

Many people felt overwhelmed and hopeless about debt. They seemed to share a sense of obligation and responsibility to repay it. But many questioned how.

In my opinion, no matter what they say about good debt or bad debt, everybody wants to get out of debt! The best kind of debt is *no debt.* Period.

Who wants to have a payment hanging over their head? Owning is better than owing, any day of the week. I'm talking about *free and clear*. That's how you build wealth and improve your quality of life.

MY BIGGEST DEBT CHALLENGE

*"I'd better get a shovel, because this debt
is going to require some serious digging!"*
—Kembala Evans

Anyone with serious debt has a story. They can tell you how they got in, what they did to get out, or why they're still in it. The only thing that may be a little cloudy is the *when*.

And I'm no different. I've been up to my eyeballs in debt. Talk about heavy! This forced me to make different choices in life (e.g., my career path).

It happened at a time that should have been filled with complete happiness. I was 21 years young and in my senior year of college. Graduation was right around the corner. I was bubbling with excitement. I couldn't wait to get out of school (who can?) and start earning some *real money*.

There was just one thing that I dreaded—my exit interview.

To say I didn't look forward to this meeting would be a major understatement. For those of you who have never heard of an exit interview, it's not a meeting to discuss your college experience. An exit interview is when you sit down with a financial aid office representative to talk about your student loans. After this meeting, you know:

- What you owe;
- When you have to start paying it back;
- Who you have to make payments to; and
- How much you have to pay every month.

They show you each and every promissory note you ever signed (yeah, those IOUs from way back when) to refresh your memory. And you'd better believe it's payback time.

In my case, I owed nearly $30,000 (roughly $29,226). This figure didn't even include my mom's PLUS student loan of approximately $8,000 that she took out to pay for my college expenses. Ouch! Somebody pinch me, because I'm having a serious nightmare here in broad daylight. Yikes!

Here's a flashback to my exit interview, after I learned exactly how much I owed in student loans:

EXIT INTERVIEW FLASHBACK STORY

FOR THOSE WHO NEED a visual, my eyes are probably popping out of my head. Boing! At this point, the financial aid representative's voice starts sounding more like Charlie Brown's teacher on *Peanuts* to me. She says, "You have to pay (wah, wah, wah…) every month."

In my mind, I'm thinking to myself, "This is SCARY! I don't even have a j-o-b yet. The monthly payment is too high!!! Student loan payment—what's she talking about?

That sounds more like a luxury car payment to me, and the payment period is twice as long."

As I look at the bottom line, I start drifting into a daze.

Then I begin thinking again . . .

"I can't stand debt. I'll probably have to work three jobs to pay these loans off in less than five years. That shouldn't be a problem though because I'm Jamaican by blood. Who am I kidding? I have to live."

Slowly, reality starts to set in. I continue thinking about the situation at hand, "OK, I need to pull myself together. Let me pick up my jaw from the floor. No need to panic!"

I try to focus on the positives. The loans aren't that bad when you look at the big picture. As a college graduate, I'll have more earning potential. Plus, I'm getting a six-month grace period and ten years to pay them back.

Still that big monthly payment is hard to digest. But she told me there are several payment options available to reduce it. They offer student loan consolidation, graduated payments, student loan forgiveness, yada, yada, yada . . . oh yeah, I can't forget about forbearance and deferment either.

While it's nice to have these options available to reduce or delay my payments, there's one BIG problem—I don't like debt! Period. And the longer I take to pay it off, the more it's going to cost me. Yikes!

In reality, I wished (pretty hard too) that my creditors would just go away. But they weren't going anywhere. So I had to find a way to pay off my student loans.

It wasn't easy. That *real money* didn't come fast. In fact, I had a stint of unemployment and underemployment (part-time and temporary jobs) after college. Despite this reality, I paid off my student loans (my mom's loan included) three years early.

You'll find out how I did it in this book. It doesn't matter if you owe more or less than I did; the fundamentals in here will help you pay off any debt. Just keep an open mind as I walk you through them step-by-step.

Now buckle up and get ready to learn how to start paying that debt down, down, down.

DON'T BEAT YOURSELF UP ABOUT PAST MISTAKES

*"Well, we all make mistakes, dear, so just
put it behind you. We should regret our mistakes
and learn from them, but never carry them
forward into the future with us."*
—L.M. Montgomery, *Anne of Avonlea*

SOME PEOPLE ARE STUCK because they can't seem to move past their mistakes. They let *their past* haunt the present and future. Don't let that be you!

Don't dwell on past mistakes and let your regret sink your hopes and dreams. You have to let go and move forward.

Think of it like this: when you make a mistake, what's done is done. More than likely, you can't go back, rewind, and erase it. So there's no need to complain, worry, or even get upset or angry about what has already happened. The only thing you can do is control your response (what happens next).

Starting today, adopt a new process for handling mistakes: accept, learn, and move on.

This strategy really helped my client (we'll call her Lucy— because everybody loves Lucy!) transform her life.

LUCY'S STORY

WHEN WE FIRST TALKED about her finances, Lucy was struggling with thousands of dollars in credit card debt. She was very unhappy. Lucy beat herself up about her past mistakes with money. Unfortunately, she always focused her energy on what she had done wrong every time.

Lucy admitted that going on extravagant vacations and buying more than she could afford were bad financial decisions. On the outside, she was living the life! In reality, Lucy couldn't afford her expensive lifestyle.

The truth is her spending habits left some bills unpaid and collection notices piling up. She felt guilty, ashamed, and helpless. The past-due bills, bank overdrafts, and collection notices in the mailbox were a huge wakeup call.

Lucy was stressed and embarrassed about her financial situation. When we talked about it, Lucy got upset and belittled herself, calling herself degrading names. Every time Lucy brought up the past, she was reliving the pain over and over again. This was emotionally draining.

Worst of all, it wasn't doing her any good. And it certainly wasn't helping the situation any.

I told Lucy that I understood how she got there. I appreciated her openness and honesty. Admitting her mistakes was a step in the right direction.

After doing a whole lot of listening I asked Lucy, "Do you want to improve your finances?" She must have thought I was crazy.

"Yes!" Lucy replied.

"Great, I can help you." I said.

Of course, a series of questions followed so I could understand the root cause of her spending issues. This discussion allowed Lucy to see the problem without blaming herself. For instance, we talked about her childhood and how she had learned about money.

After our talk, I encouraged Lucy to learn from her past mistakes. It's important to learn the lesson, so you don't have to repeat it. She came to understand this concept and we never looked back. We made the shift to be solution focused together.

We created her financial goals and a debt-free action plan to achieve them. I'm happy to say that her attitude about everything improved. Instead of beating herself up about the past, she embraced it. And she worked mighty hard to change her future.

Lucy made smarter financial decisions (e.g., cut spending, budgeted money, stuck to her plan) independently. She dared to be different and did not give into the peer pressure around her to spend more. Sometimes those pressures can come from places that you least expect it like our friends and family. They can add pressure on us when they tell us what we should be buying or doing with our own money. Fortunately, Lucy identified this problem. And she did not let the words of others cloud her vision.

After a few short years of focused effort, hard work, and perseverance, Lucy achieved every goal. In fact, she had a new attitude and shared her experience with others to let them know change is possible. And that's a beautiful thing!

CHANGE IS POSSIBLE

To fix any problem, you need to understand it. You can start with a self-reflection. A few questions to consider:

- What happened?
- How did I get into debt?
- What can I do to stay out of debt (e.g., budget, use cash only)?

Taking the time to understand what went wrong will help you learn the lesson, so you can move forward without making the same mistakes.

You have to be willing to:

- **Accept it** (what's done is done)
- **Learn from it** (there is always a lesson)
- **Move on** (apply what you learned to achieve success)

It's important to remember that everyone makes mistakes. No one is perfect. Besides, mistakes can be great teachers. They teach us *what not to do*. Be sure to learn the lesson or you're bound to repeat it.

If you can't let go of past mistakes, please learn to let go and forgive yourself. You can do this! You've gotta be willing to move on to change tomorrow.

Now that you've stopped beating yourself up, let's go to the next step.

> *"Mistakes are the stepping stones to wisdom.*
> *We learn from trial and error; we become*
> *wise by understanding problems."*
> —Leon Brown

MIND OVER DEBT

*"Progress is impossible without change, and those who
cannot change their minds cannot change anything."*
—George Bernard Shaw

THE MOST POWERFUL TOOL you have is *your mind*. It's true. After all, your mind controls everything you do.

Ultimately, thoughts fuel your actions. You thought about reading this book before you ever read one word. You made up your mind to read it and your actions followed. Right?

Some of the greatest inventions hatched from a simple idea or thought. These ideas led ordinary people to make life-changing inventions, such as electricity, cars, traffic lights, and airplanes.

Your mind is very powerful. It can take you where you want to be or keep you trapped where you've always been. So why not use your mind to help you get rid of debt?

SURVIVING BRRRY COLD CHICAGO WINTERS

I was born and raised in the sunshine state of Florida. So when people back home heard I lived in Chicago, they had to ask, "How do you handle the brutally cold weather?"

My response usually surprised them. I'd just say, "It's mental."

"Ugghh. OK." They often replied in disbelief.

I believe anything is possible with the right mindset. Of course, you must use common sense. I never went outside in frigid temperatures wearing shorts. I prepared myself mentally and physically (coat, gloves, and hat) for the cold weather.

When you know what to expect, you can prepare for it. It's really that simple.

I remember when we first moved from Florida to Chicago. It was the end of December, and my oldest daughter was only a year old at the time. As soon as we stepped off the plane, she could feel the difference instantly.

Her response was actually funny. And she quickly picked up three new words that winter: snow, cold, and jacket. I couldn't believe how quickly she put it together.

You see, when you get your mind right, everything else follows.

MAKE UP YOUR MIND

"Human beings, by changing the inner attitudes of their minds, can change the outer aspects of their lives."
—William James

Have you made up your mind to become debt-free yet? Your answer to this question could determine whether you succeed or fail. Let me tell you why.

I've witnessed time and time again just how important what you think is. That's why my personal motto is, "If you can perceive it, just believe it, and you will achieve it."

Let's take a closer look at this motto. "If you can perceive it"—**To perceive it,** you have to see it. So, visualize your success first. Countless studies have shown the effectiveness of visualization. In fact, it's been proven to produce better results in a variety of areas.

That's why I asked you to *imagine yourself debt-free* earlier in the introduction. If you missed it, please go back and read it. It's a great exercise to help get you started.

You must have a vision for "where you want to be." It's easier to accomplish something when you can see yourself doing it. As Stephen Covey wrote in *The 7 Habits of Highly Successful People*, you want to "begin with the end in mind."[1] So, get a clear picture of what you want to achieve now.

---

1 Covey, Stephen R., *The 7 Habits of Highly Effective People*, (New York: Fireside, 1990), 97.

Visualization is a powerful mental exercise to help you achieve your goals. For example, I heard about a basketball team that put this theory to the test on the court.

The basketball team divided itself into two groups. The first group practiced shooting the ball on the court physically, while the other group practiced their shots mentally. No basketball or hoop. They only visualized themselves making basketball shots.

When they finally played a game, the group who practiced using the visualization technique had the better field goal shooting percentage. In other words, the players who shot the ball in their minds actually made more baskets than the players who did not. This is a simple example of how using our mental capabilities can deliver stronger results.

Visualization can be powerful in many areas of your life. In fact, it's been used in a variety of professional fields (medical, entrepreneur, astronauts) to achieve better outcomes. Why don't you put the power of visualization to the test for yourself? Start seeing yourself doing what you want to do. You may be amazed at the results.

Next, you must **believe it's possible**.

Many people have achieved extraordinary things because they believed it was possible. No matter what others may have thought or said, they knew they could do it. And it's that unwavering faith that has led to life's greatest achievements.

"I am the greatest, I said that even before I knew I was."
—Muhammad Ali

For example, let's go back to 1961. In a speech on May 25, when President John F. Kennedy said, "I believe that this nation should commit itself to achieving the goal, before this decade is out, of landing a man on the moon and returning him safely to the Earth."

That was a bold statement and a clear vision. President Kennedy proposed *something that had never been done.* Have you ever looked at the moon? It's mighty far away from Earth. According to NASA it's about 238,855 miles away. Despite this fact, President Kennedy believed his goal could be achieved.

Still, there were many people who never believed it would happen. Some of those doubters were probably sitting right there in Congress when he spoke those very words too.

Surely there were some believers out there. After all, a team of people worked awfully hard to achieve that goal. On July 20, 1969, President Kennedy's goal was reached when Neil Armstrong took the first steps on the moon. It was a historical moment indeed.

Whether you're aiming for the moon or anything else in life, **you have to believe to achieve**. Besides, if you don't believe, who will?

CHANGE YOUR MINDSET, CHANGE YOUR LIFE

Do you have the right mindset? This is probably one of the toughest hurdles people face when trying to achieve their goals. For example, some people want to save money. But they think it's impossible. They truly believe this. They tell me it's too hard to save. They don't make enough money. They never learned how to save.

They are absolutely convinced of their limitations. And they don't save a dime. Could they be setting themselves up for failure or limiting themselves with their thinking?

Remember, our minds are very powerful. If you say to yourself, "I can't save," then you are limiting yourself with your thought and words. You could be doing this without even realizing it. And as a result, your actions will find every other use for your money except savings.

This is a "can't do" attitude at work. More than likely, to start saving, these people just need to change their words and attitudes about it. Then they will be more open and creative about finding ways to save.

Having a positive "can do" attitude makes a big difference. It can change everything. And, suddenly, these same people are no longer standing on the sidelines in despair. They are in the game and building up savings.

That's the power of the mind. It changes things. It's almost like flipping on a light switch and *watching the impossible become possible*.

But it all starts with you. Real change comes from the inside out. **With the right mindset, you'll achieve success. Your thoughts, words, and attitude must be in complete alignment.**

It really is mental. And you're in complete control. Once you put your mind over debt, everything else will follow.

It's important to stay positive about paying off your debt. Avoid talking negative. Stay focused on the end goal— becoming debt-free.

No matter what your goal is in life, you have to see it as possible. Believe you can do it. And put in the work to make it happen. That's a real formula for success.

> *"So much in life is mental. Sometimes we lose the race before we even step on the track. It's all because we knew we would. Shift your mindset."*
> —Kembala Evans

SET YOUR GOALS

"People with goals succeed because they know
where they are going . . . It's as simple as that."
—Earl Nightingale

NOW THAT YOU have your mind right, it's time to set your goals. Goal setting is a crucial step to achieve success. Each goal is like a stepping-stone on your path to financial freedom.

That being said, creating goals will require you to think through the actions needed to become debt-free. What will you need to do to reach your goals? How will you go about doing it?

You may be asking yourself, "Why do I have to create goals? It's a waste of time. I already know my goal—it's to be debt-free." That's a start, but what steps will you need to take to make it happen?

I strongly encourage you to invest the time to create your goals. You may want to be debt-free, but it's not enough to know. You must think through what you need to do to become debt-free. Setting goals allows you to break everything down into smaller steps, so they are easier to handle and achieve individually.

Many studies have shown that goal setting works. A Dominican University of California study revealed up to a 76 percent achievement rate when goals are set early on.[2]

Ready to set your goals? Here are some tips to help you:

1. **Write Your Goals Down.** People who write their goals down have a higher probability of reaching them. Some people have claimed to have seen a 90% goal achievement rate when they are written down. There's something special that happens when you physically write them down—not type them. Perhaps it has to do with the left and right side of the brain. Who knows? Just write them down. You can type them up later.

2. **Be Specific.** You need to be explicit about what you want to achieve. What actions do you need to take to become debt-free? Say you have an auto loan, credit cards, and student loans. Break down every goal to be specific about when you'll pay off each debt.

---

2 "Study Focuses on Strategies for Achieving Goals, Resolutions." Dominican University of California. Accessed November 22, 2019. https://www.dominican.edu/dominicannews/ study-highlights-strategies-for-achieving-goals.

3. **Make it Measureable.** Creating measureable goals allows you to monitor your progress. How are you doing? Are you on track to reach your goal?

4. **Be Realistic.** Set a goal that is achievable. This helps keep you motivated. As you start reaching your goals, stretch yourself and add more challenging goals.

5. **Set a Target Date.** Without a date, you have nothing to aim for. Your goal must be time bound. When do you want to accomplish your goal?

6. **List Actions.** Once you've written your goal down, think through the actions you must take to reach it. What steps will you need to take to achieve your goal? Write down the actions needed for every goal.

An example of a goal might be: Pay off credit card Z by the end of the year.

Actions:

- Call credit card Z to negotiate a lower interest rate.
- Create a payment plan to meet this goal.
- Make a $120 payment every month.

KEEP YOUR GOALS IN FRONT OF YOU

The last thing you want to do is write your goals on some random piece of paper, never to be seen again. That would completely defeat the purpose. You didn't invest the time writing your goals down to do that.

No, you're too focused. You're so laser-sharp focused that you will always keep your goals top of mind. You might choose to review them weekly, biweekly, or monthly to see how you are progressing.

For those of you determined to succeed, you may take it a step further and look at your goals every day. I had a client who taped his debt-free goals on the refrigerator, so he saw them every time he went to the fridge. Then there are people who tape them on their bathroom mirrors or ceilings (they must have low ceilings or some really big handwriting), so they can see them morning and night. Do whatever works best for you.

I remember a coworker of mine that had a creative way of keeping her goal out in front of her. I noticed it on her desk. She had a picture of some high-end Viking kitchen appliances taped on her computer monitor. I asked her why she taped that picture there. She told me it served as a constant reminder and motivator for her goal to buy those appliances one day. Brilliant! She posted her goal right in the place where she spent the majority of her day. As a computer programmer, what better place could she put it than on the computer?

VISUALIZE YOUR SUCCESS

We discussed the importance of visualization in the last step. Take a look at your goals and visualize yourself accomplishing each and every one of them. Think about how it will feel when you actually realize your goal has been accomplished.

As Albert Einstein once said, *"Imagination is everything. It is the preview of life's coming attractions."* That pretty much sums it up. Start seeing your life the way you want it to be.

DISCOVER THE X FACTOR FOR GOAL ACHIEVEMENT

Do you want to know the secret sauce to achieving your goals? Finding an accountability partner to help you achieve your goals could make all the difference. An accountability partner is someone who holds you accountable for reaching your goals.

This person should be someone you trust. Some people to consider are:

- a close friend,
- significant other,
- family member,
- coach, or
- anyone who can encourage and motivate you to do your best.

Once you've identified this person, ask if he or she is willing to be your accountability partner. Perhaps the two of you could work together to help each other achieve success. Be sure to communicate what you are looking for in an accountability partner to get his or her commitment.

Share your goals when you first meet with your accountability partner. And discuss the actions you will take to achieve them. This discussion will also give you an opportunity to discuss any concerns you have with someone you trust who can provide guidance and encouragement.

Schedule a regular time (weekly, monthly) to meet or provide an update to your accountability partner on your progress. Your partner is there to give you support, but you'll be the one working to achieve the goals. Always remember, "If it's to be, it's up to me."

Finally, **never quit**. If it's not working, try again in a different way. It's your determination and persistence that will get you there.

When you reach your goal, set a new one. Keep challenging yourself to reach higher and higher.

> *"What you get by achieving your goals*
> *is not as important as what you become*
> *by achieving your goals."*
> —Henry David Thoreau

CREATE YOUR DEBT-FREE ACTION PLAN

*"Create a definite plan for carrying out your desire,
and begin at once, whether you're ready or not,
to put it into action."*
– Napoleon Hill

ROADMAPS MAKE IT easy to get from point A to point B. Without a roadmap you might find yourself driving around in circles and wasting life's most precious resource—time.

I think map apps and GPS devices are some of the most useful inventions around. It's nice to get turn-by-turn directions at the click of a button. Talk about convenience.

This also gives my confidence a little boost because I don't have a strong sense of direction. With turn-by-turn navigation, I don't have to stop and ask for directions. Best of all, it *saves me time and money.*

I'd like for you to think of your debt-free action plan the same way. It will show you how to get from point A (in debt) to point B (out of debt) easier. With a plan in hand, you can see what you need to do to drop the debt weight. In this step, you'll learn how to build a debt-free action plan to help you save time and money.

Before you create your debt-free action plan, you'll need to know:

- Who you owe (creditors)
- How much you owe (balances)
- What it's costing you (e.g., interest rates, fees)

GATHER YOUR DEBT INFORMATION

You can start gathering this information from your monthly billing statements. Contact your creditor if you're unable to find the account information (interest rate, balance) on your bill. The creditor should be able to provide you with the account details (balance, interest rate, terms).

To make sure you have a complete picture of your outstanding debts, pull your credit report. Your credit report shows you a list of any accounts that have been reported to the credit companies.

Pulling your credit report won't cost you anything. It's free. By law, the credit reporting companies (Equifax, Experian, TransUnion) are required to give you a free copy of your credit report every year.

You may request your free credit report online at AnnualCreditReport.com. This site also offers additional products and services for a fee. **Just say no to the additional offers, and get your free credit report.** It's fast and easy; I got mine in less than five minutes. You can also call 877-322-8228 to order a free copy of your credit report.

Beware of imposter websites that try to lure you in with a free credit report offer. Other sites may require you to sign up for products and services to receive your credit report. Your annual credit report should be FREE, without any strings attached. So you don't have to enroll in any other paid services (i.e. credit monitoring) to get your free credit report.

Finally, when gathering your debt information, be sure to include any personal IOUs.

CREDIT MANAGEMENT TIPS:

1. Pay your bills on-time and pay down debt to help improve your credit score.

2. Monitor your credit for free year round by requesting a free credit report from a different credit company every four months. For example, request a free credit report from Equifax in January, Experian in May, and TransUnion in September.

3. If you find any errors on your credit report, contact the company who reported it to discuss the problem and try to have it resolved. Notify the credit reporting company about any issues or concerns also. Be sure to follow their process for filing a dispute, including as much information as possible. The instructions for filing a dispute are available on each credit company's website:

   - Equifax: http://www.equifax.com
   - Experian: http://www.experian.com
   - TransUnion: http://www.transunion.com

CREATE YOUR DEBT-FREE ACTION PLAN

You can create your debt-free action plan using a notepad, word processor, or spreadsheet. For those of you using personal finance software like Quicken, check the options they have available to create your plan. Use a system that works best for you to manage your plan.

What to include on your debt-free action plan:

- **Creditor Name:** List the name of each company or person owed.
- **Priority Number:** Use this column to prioritize your accounts based on your payoff strategy. We'll discuss this shortly.
- **Interest Rate:** This is the current interest rate you are paying on the account.
- **Outstanding Balance:** This is the amount owed on the account when you start your plan. Use the most up-to-date information available.
- **Minimum Monthly Payment:** List the minimum payment amount required on the account. Keep in mind this minimum payment amount must be paid every month.
- **Monthly Payment:** This is the amount you'll pay on your account every month.
- **Credit Limit:** This is the credit you have available on the account. Your balance should not exceed your credit limit. If it does, you'll need to make paying it down below your credit limit a high priority to avoid additional fees.
- **Notes:** Document any important account details, such as a special 0% interest rate that expires on a specific date (e.g. six months). Include any important notes about your account payoff strategy, which we'll discuss next.

Be sure to list this information for every outstanding debt you owe. This will help ensure you take everything into account when you lay out your payoff strategy.

DEVELOP YOUR PAYOFF STRATEGY

Now that you've created your debt-free action plan, you need to have a strategy to pay off your debt. Which account will you pay off first? How will you decide?

There are two proven methods commonly used to attack debt:

- **Debt Stacking****—This strategy organizes debt based on the interest rate. The target account is the one with the highest interest rate, as it costs you the most.
- **Debt Snowball****—This strategy organizes debt based on the amount of money owed (account balance). The first target account is the one with the lowest account balance. This strategy is often chosen for those who need to see results faster.

> ****IMPORTANT NOTE:** While you'll pay more toward your target account, you must continue to make the minimum payment due on all of your accounts. Making on-time payments and paying down debt helps your credit score.

I normally recommend the debt stacking payoff strategy. I prefer this method because it allows you to pay down debt faster. Plus, when you pay off the highest interest account, you save more money.

But debt stacking doesn't work for everyone, especially when that first account has a large balance. Some people are more motivated when they pay off smaller balances first using the debt snowball. This gives them a sense of accomplishment that inspires them to keep going. For these people, the debt snowball is a better fit.

Choose the payoff strategy that works best for you. Be sure to take into account any special-case scenarios (over-the-credit-limit accounts, promotional interest rate expiring) when selecting your approach. Special situations like a 0% interest rate offer expiring may require you to prioritize your accounts differently.

For example, I worked with someone who had a 90-day same-as-cash deal on a credit card purchase. On paper, his account had a 0% interest rate. But, it came with strings attached, he had to pay it off within 90 days to avoid a 24% high-interest rate charge. If the entire balance is not paid in full in 90 days, then the total deferred interest amount is charged on the next billing statement. This amount is calculated based on the original purchase date amount—no matter what the current balance on the account is since it wasn't paid in full.

Given his situation, he made the 90-day same-as-cash credit card his first target account. He chose the debt stacking method for the rest of his accounts. This strategy worked best for him.

Just like he did, you'll have to determine the right strategy given your specific circumstances.

Table 1 shows how a debt-free action plan might look:

Creditor	Priority #	Interest Rate	Outstanding Balance	Minimum Payment	Monthly Payment	Notes
Credit Card A	2	17.50%	$2,288	$45	$45	
Credit Card B	1	22.99%	$4,614	$94	$300	They will not lower interest rate.
Auto Loan	3	7.90%	$9,567	$425	$425	Look into refinancing for a lower interest rate.

Table 1

This person is using the debt stacking option. The extra money is being applied on the first target account (Credit Card B) to pay it down faster. She is still paying the minimum monthly payment on every other account.

After Credit Card B has been paid off, Credit Card A is the next target account. Now she will pay $345 every month on Credit Card A. And she will continue to pay the minimum payment on her auto loan, which is $425.

Table 2 shows how all of the money that was previously used to pay down Credit Card B will now be applied to Credit Card A:

Creditor	Priority #	Interest Rate	Outstanding Balance	Minimum Payment	Monthly Payment	Notes
Credit Card A	1	17.50%	$1,787	$45	$345	
Auto Loan	2	7.90%	$6,839	$425	$425	Unable to refinance auto loan.

Table 2

UPDATE YOUR ACTION PLAN AND GET TO WORK

After you've decided on a payoff strategy that works for you, update your action plan to support it:

1. Prioritize your accounts (e.g., target one, target two . . .).
2. Update your plan details (i.e. monthly payment amounts).
3. Add any special notes on your accounts (if needed).

Review your debt-free action plan and monthly billing statements every month. Use your plan to manage any changes to your accounts (interest rates, payoff strategy). Take action! Stay committed to your plan and watch your balances drop. It's a great motivator to see the results of hard work!

> *"Perseverance is my motto."*
> —Madam C. J. Walker

PAY DOWN DEBT FASTER

"That which we persist in doing becomes easier to do,
not that the nature of the thing has changed
but that our power to do has increased."
—Ralph Waldo Emerson

THERE'S NO EASY way out of debt. You can't snap your fingers and say, "Debt, be gone." And then poof! The debt just disappears.

I wish it were that easy. But the truth is, you are going to have to be determined and take some serious action to make the debt go away.

One thing's for sure: if you're only paying the minimum payment on high-balance and high-interest credit card debt, it could take you years or even decades to pay it off.

If you don't believe me, take a closer look at your credit card statement. Most credit card statements have a "Minimum

Payment Warning," which warns you about how paying the minimum only costs more money in interest and takes longer to pay off. Your statement may provide an example of this using a small table to show you an estimate of how much time it will take to pay off your current balance and how much it would cost you.

In this step, you'll learn some techniques you can use to eliminate debt faster.

These are the same strategies I used to get rid of more than $20,000 of debt in less than seven months. And my clients put them into action to achieve life-changing results. They've paid off high-interest credit cards, auto loans, student loans, mortgages, and home equity loans. I love hearing everyday people use these proven techniques to eliminate debt.

"Do the best you can until you know better.
Then when you know better, do better."
—Maya Angelou

For example, I helped one of my clients eliminate over $20,000 in student loans and $10,000 in credit card debt in a few years. That shot his credit score up from a 532 (a 'poor' credit rating) to over 700 (a 'good' credit rating). I only remember this because he was so embarrassed and upset when he first shared his credit report with me. Today, decades later he is proud to have a credit score in the 800s (an 'excellent' rating) because he continues to practice good debt management skills.

If we can get rid of debt, then so can YOU. You may even do it faster. Who knows?

This is one step you will definitely want to read again. As you'll soon see, it's packed with useful tips to drop the debt weight.

12 WAYS TO PAY DOWN DEBT FASTER

1. Stop Worrying and Start Doing

Being in debt can take you on an emotional roller coaster that makes you want to—**do nothing**. Are you feeling stuck in a rut? If so, I encourage you to *start doing*. When you do, you'll see there is light at the end of the tunnel. You can fix it.

If you're too depressed to muster up any energy, I urge you to read Dale Carnegie's book *How to Stop Worrying and Start Living*. Also, check out the American Psychological Association's stress management tips and consider talking to someone you trust about your feelings.[3]

2. When You're Drowning in Debt, Stop Going Down!

You can't keep doing the same thing and expect different results. *You must change what you're doing to get better results.* Practicing self-control, discipline, and delayed gratification (the art of patience can do wonders for your wallet) will help you spend less and pay down debt more quickly. Better yet,

---

3   "Healthy Ways to Handle Life's Stressors." American Psychological Association. November 1, 2019. https://www.apa.org/topics/content/stress-tips.

take a close look at your spending habits and live below your means.

For more information on how you can improve your money management skills, check out my book *Get Your Money Right*. It offers you tips to live below your means and shows you how to avoid the psychological triggers that often cause us to fall into the debt trap.

3. Use Cash

Paying cash should help curb your spending habits. There's something about using paper and coins that makes us think a little harder about our purchasing decisions. In fact, it's been proven that people spend less with cash.

Are you spending too much money using credit cards? If so, consider using cash or your debit card instead. You may want to shred your credit cards or limit them to only special occasions, such as travel.

4. Prioritize Needs Over Wants

Do you really *need* that? Making sacrifices and downsizing your lifestyle will help you find extra cash to pay down debt. Simple things like downgrading or eliminating your cable package, bundling up services, and shopping smarter can help you reduce your expenses. The more money you save, the more you'll have to pay off your debt.

5. Control Your Spending

Want to find out where your money is going? Track your spending for a month. Write down everything you spend money on every day. This exercise can be a very eye-opening experience.

When you have a better idea of your spending habits, it's easier to create a budget. Your budget will show you what's coming in and going out every month. You can use a budget to help you manage your money better, reduce expenses, and reach your financial goals.

Creating a budget is easy. Simply use a piece of paper or worksheet. To get started, type "create a budget" into your favorite search engine to find step-by-step instructions. There are also free online tools, apps, and spreadsheets you can use. Some popular budgeting software and online tools are:

- Mint.com
- Mvelopes
- Quicken
- YNAB (You Need a Budget)
- Plus an honorable mention to help your money grow— Acorns

Find a system that works for you to control spending. Another option is to use the cash envelope system. This is when you set aside money for specific purposes. For instance, you put $75 in an envelope every month for eating out. When that money runs out, you can't eat out again until the next month.

6. Increase Your Income

Sometimes the only answer is you need more money to dig out of debt. Consider taking on a part-time job or a side hustle, looking for a higher paying job, or somehow creating more income streams to pay down debt.

For those who collect a big refund during tax season every year, you may be able to increase your take-home pay by changing your W-4. This will decrease your annual refund but increase your paychecks in the meantime, so you can pay your debts now. Check out the IRS.gov withholding calculator or consult a tax professional to find out if this is the right answer for you.

7. Use Extra Cash, Cash Windfalls, Savings, and Non-Retirement Investments

When a raise or a cash windfall comes, debt repayment is often low on the priority list. But, once we've made up our minds to be debt free, we understand that delaying our vacation getaway or a new device will help put us closer to our goal. Besides, life's better without the financial headaches afterward.

Some of us never think of touching savings or investments to pay down debt. I've been there myself; this was my "duh" moment. But we must carefully consider these options too. Have you ever looked at the interest rate you're earning on your savings account? Take a look at it. Then compare it to how much money you are paying in interest on that credit card statement? More than likely, you're paying a lot more interest than you're earning. If you have more than six months of expenses in your emergency savings fund or investments (excluding retirement accounts), you could use a portion to pay down high-interest debt. After you pay off your debts, start putting money back into your savings and investments. That's how you'll make your money grow.

8. Negotiate Lower Interest Rates and Consider Refinancing Loans

A lower interest rate could help you make a real dent in your debt. Of course, it's easier to talk with your lender about lowering the interest rate when you pay on time. What interest rate should you ask for? Check out bankrate.com or creditcards.com to find reasonable credit card interest rates. Be sure to mention any enticing competitor credit card offers you've received as leverage. Call your lender and ask for a lower interest rate. Remember the golden question is always—is that the best you can do?

Sometimes people have ridiculously high interest rates on their loans. For example, I heard a story about a young man who went into the car dealership to buy a new car. He was so excited about qualifying for the loan that he signed the contract without an interest rate. He later discovered they charged him a whopping 25% in interest.

So, should I refinance my loan? It depends. If I were that young man, I'd definitely be shopping around to get a lower interest rate car loan. Pronto!

Refinancing your loan may be a viable option to help you save more money. Of course, you will have to do a cost benefit analysis to see if it is right for you. Be sure to compare the credit terms (repayment period, interest rate, any benefits) and costs (any fees). There are plenty of online tools and calculators to help you analyze whether refinancing your loan is the right answer for you.

9. Sell Stuff You Don't Need or Want

Is your car note weighing you down? Consider downgrading to get something more affordable, if selling your car makes financial sense. Also, old stuff in the garage that's taking up space could be turned into dollars. Garage sales and online sales/auctions are great ways to turn stuff into cash. Before you sell, make sure you know the value of what you have, so you can make the most money for your possessions. Get a professional appraisal for any valuable property like art, jewelry, watches, and rugs.

> **IMPORTANT NOTE:** When selling items online (e.g., Craigslist), be careful and protect yourself. There are a lot of scams out there. Some buyers may even set sellers up to steal the merchandise. To avoid these types of issues, arrange to meet the buyer/seller in a busy public place. With these types of crimes on the rise, special police units are advising you to complete your transaction online and mail it. If you have to meet in person, then choose a safe place like your local police station.

10. Make Biweekly Payments

Interest is often calculated daily, so you can save more money when you split your monthly payment in half and pay every two weeks. This is a great way to squeeze in an extra payment every year. For example, say your car payment is $500 a month and is due on the 20th. You'd pay the first half ($250) on the 1st. Then you'd pay the rest ($250) on the 15th. Using this strategy, you'd continue to pay $250 every other week and $6,500 per year instead of $6,000. That's one extra payment a year.

> **IMPORTANT NOTE: Check with your lender to make sure it's OK to pay every two weeks before you start making biweekly payments.** Always pay the full amount due before the due date. If you decide to use automatic payments, set them up yourself with your financial institution to avoid any lender setup fees.

11. Balance Transfers or Debt Consolidation Loans

If you're dealing with high-interest credit card debt, a balance transfer or personal loan could be a great opportunity to save. But you have to do the cost benefit analysis first.

Some questions to consider on balance transfer: What's the promotional rate? How long does it last? What happens after it expires? How much are the transfer fees? If you decide to do a balance transfer, you must be disciplined with the additional credit. Remember, the goal is to get rid of debt.

Personal loans often offer you a much lower interest rate and a fixed repayment schedule. This may be an option for those with "good credit" who receive a great interest rate. Keep in mind this is a loan, so make sure you are comfortable with the monthly payments, repayment schedule, and the terms of the agreement.

12. Ask for Help

If you need help, consider contacting the National Foundation for Credit Counseling (NFCC) for assistance at NFCC.org or 800-388-2227. NFCC provides low-cost credit counseling services.

Addicted to debt? Debtors Anonymous may be able to help you. Visit www.debtorsanonymous.org for more information.

> *"The three great essentials to achieve*
> *anything worthwhile are, first, hard work; second,*
> *stick-to-itiveness; third, common sense."*
> —Thomas A. Edison

WATCH YOUR DEBT

"When your debt drops down, your spirits go up."
—Kembala Evans

YOU'RE ALMOST THERE. So far, we've discussed some powerful strategies and tools to achieve success:

- **Let Go of Past Mistakes** - Accept, learn, and move on.
- **Mind Over Debt** - Visualize your success, believe in yourself, and have a positive can-do attitude.
- **Set Your Goals** - What? When? How?
- **Create Your Debt-Free Action Plan** - Lay out your plan and strategy to become debt-free.
- **Pay Down Debt Faster** - Take ACTION! Be committed and creative about achieving your goals.

And we're not done yet. This step is the one that could be the most motivating. I want you to *measure your results*. Just like a person trying to lose weight steps on a scale to see how many pounds he's lost, you need to monitor your account balances to see how much they've dropped.

Numbers never lie.

They will show you if your hard work is paying off (no pun intended). Will you reach your goal? If not, why? What can you do to improve your results? The only way to answer these questions is to watch your debt.

How else would you track your progress? **To do this, add a "Current Balance" column on your debt-free action plan as shown in Table 3. And update this column every time you make a payment on your account. That's right, every time you make a payment, track the new balance amount.**

When I was on my debt-free journey, this step really pushed me the most. I loved watching my balances go down, down, down! It inspired me to be more creative and aggressive about eliminating debt. In fact, I made extra payments just to see it go lower and lower. It was incredible to watch, especially when those balances hit the magic number $0.

For instance, say you owe $9,575 on a car loan. After six months of hard work, you cut the balance in half, to $4,788. Your plan is finally working. Now you can see the finish line. This pushes you a little harder, and you end up paying it off much earlier than you expected. It feels good and liberating, especially when it's finally paid off and you hold that car title in your hands. Ownership is a wonderful feeling!

Yes, paid in full. No more payments. No more bills. No more installment coupon books (oops, I probably dated myself with that one). It just makes you want to do the happy dance like an NFL player in the end zone after a big touchdown.

This is what you have to look forward to. So what are you waiting for? Start watching your debt today. It's easy to do and worth every minute. Believe me. The results could be amazing.

Table 3 shows how you can use the "Current Balance" column to monitor your success:

Creditor	Priority #	Interest Rate	Outstanding Balance	Minimum Payment	Monthly Payment	Current Balance	Notes
Student Loan	1	5.45%	$22,345	$405	$1,050	$12,825	Last one, I've got this!

Table 3

"I often say that paying off your debt is
like dieting. There are no miracle cures;
it takes discipline and hard work."
—Lisa Madigan

CELEBRATE YOUR SUCCESSES! (WAAAHOO!)

*"Celebrate your achievements. And be like the
Energizer bunny and keep going . . ."*
—Kembala Evans

THE LAST STEP is the easiest. Read closely, because it's so short you might miss it. Here goes: *reward yourself for your successes.*

You've done the work. So take a little time to celebrate your achievements, whether that's paying off a target account or reaching one of your goals. Do something special to mark the moment.

You don't have to do anything elaborate. It can be small. But, given all of your hard work and efforts, you deserve to celebrate your accomplishment!

TEN WAYS TO CELEBRATE YOUR SUCCESS WITHOUT BREAKING THE BANK

1. Go on YouTube and play Kool & the Gang's "Celebration." Dance, sing, and shout for free.
2. Have your favorite dessert. Enjoy each and every bite. Delish!
3. Take some "me" time and do nothing. Give yourself a pat on the back, too.
4. Kick back and enjoy your favorite movie.
5. Get out and smell the roses. Go ahead and take a victory stroll outside!
6. Make a video just for you. In the video, you can reflect on what you did, how it feels, and what you're going to do next.
7. Take your accountability partner out to lunch.
8. Go to your favorite restaurant with happy hour specials. Indulge in tasty half-price appetizers.
9. Frame your last statement showing it's paid off ($0 balance). Keep it as a constant reminder of your achievement.
10. Spend the day enjoying your favorite hobby or sport on a budget.

If you have any other low-cost ideas to celebrate success, please send them my way via Twitter @Kembala or contact me at kembala.com. I'd love to see any of the videos you've made on your debt-free journey too.

> *"I never dreamed about success, I worked for it."*
> —Estee Lauder

STAY FOCUSED ON YOUR END GOAL

"Knowing Is Not Enough; We Must Apply.
Wishing Is Not Enough; We Must Do."
—Johann Wolfgang Von Goethe

I ENCOURAGE YOU to *stay focused* on the end goal—becoming debt-free. You can "Make it Happen." But **taking action** is crucial to your success. In fact, nothing changes without it.

There may be times when you feel discouraged. That's the time to dig down deep and find the courage to press on. Remember, real change comes from within. It's your persistence and determination that will get you there.

A few parting thoughts to put you on the path to financial freedom:

LEARN FROM PAST MISTAKES. Experience is a great teacher. After all, it's through failure that we achieve success. Apply the knowledge you've gained to make better financial decisions every day for a brighter tomorrow.

VISUALIZE YOUR SUCCESS. How does your success look to you? Can you see it? Can you feel it? Imagination is everything!

BE POSITIVE. Have a "can do" attitude. Think and speak positive. Optimism paves the way for more desirable outcomes.

PRACTICE GOOD MONEY MANAGEMENT HABITS. Take control of your money. Creating a budget and sticking to it will help you do this. Be a disciplined spender. Some people use a spending journal to keep a close eye on their money.

SHOP SMARTER. Who wants to keep buying the same thing over and over? Not me. Be a value shopper. Use a shopping list to prioritize needs over wants. Avoid impulse purchases. Shop around for the best deal and save money with coupons.

THINK DIFFERENT. Forget about keeping up with the Joneses, giving in to peer pressure, and living a lie. Stand in your truth and buy what you can afford. Reject the "buy now, pay later" philosophy. Be frugal and enjoy life.

DON'T QUIT. Sure, you may be sitting on a mountain of debt right now. But once you get moving, you'll be chipping away at it in no time. Don't give up! Stay focused and committed.

SAVE FOR TOMORROW. Plan for tomorrow. As Benjamin Franklin said, "If you fail to plan, you are planning to fail!" So fund an emergency savings fund with at least six months of your monthly expenses. Be proactive about saving for your retirement too. Invest wisely and consider seeking professional investment advice from a Certified Financial Planner (CFP).

I wish you the best on your debt-free journey. Enjoy it! I'd love to hear from you. Feel free to reach out to me at kembala.com.

Thank you for reading this book! If you've found it to be of value, please spread the word, leave a book review, or buy someone a copy.

Best wishes,

Kembala

P.S. When it comes to personal finance, get personal, because it's your money and no one will ever care more about it than you.

> *"Money is a tool. It will take you wherever you wish,*
> *but it will not replace you as the driver."*
> —Ayn Rand

BONUS MATERIALS

REAL TALK ON STUDENT LOANS

"Debt certainly isn't always a bad thing. A mortgage can
help you afford a home. Student loans can be a necessity
in getting a good job. Both are investments worth making,
and both come with fairly low interest rates."
—Jean Chatzky, personal finance journalist

GOT STUDENT LOAN DEBT? You're not alone. In 2019, it's estimated that over 43 million Americans young and old have
student loan debt.

According to the New York Federal Reserve's *Quarterly*
Report on Household Debt and Credit (third quarter of
2019) there is now $1.50 trillion dollars in student loan debt
outstanding.[4] The only debt that surpasses student loans is
mortgage debt. Given these startling numbers, you probably
know someone with student loan debt. It may even be you.

---

4   "HHDC_2019Q3." Federal Reserve Bank of New York. November
     2019. https://www.newyorkfed.org/medialibrary/interactives/house-
     holdcredit/data/pdf/HHDC_2019Q3.pdf.

Student loan debt is impacting people of all ages and backgrounds across the country. The truth of the matter is that celebrities (Kerry Washington, Miles Teller, Kate Walsh), politicians on the left and the right (President Barack Obama, Senator Ted Cruz, Senator Marco Rubio), and everyday people like you and me all know how it feels to be saddled with student loan debt.

Here's what Former President Barack Obama said about student loans:

Michelle and I, we're only where we are today because scholarships and student loans gave us a shot at a great education. And we know a little bit about trying to pay back student loans, too, because we didn't come from a wealthy family. So we each graduated from college and law school with a mountain of debt. And even though we got good jobs, we barely finished paying it off just before I was elected to the U.S. Senate. ... I mean, I was in my 40s when we finished paying off our debt.

Anyone who has struggled with student loan debt has a story. Hundreds of student loan borrowers sounded off about their own experiences in my "Student Loan Debt in America" survey (2019). It's no joke! Some of those enormous balances can make you want to scream or ball yourself up into the fetal position and cry your eyes out.

It gets worse. Some parents carry large amounts of student loan debt for their children's education. They obtain these loans just to help their kids pay for college. And while they don't earn a degree themselves, they end up bearing the hefty cost of that education in their own names.

WHY STUDENT LOAN DEBT MATTERS

I openly shared my biggest debt challenge in the introduction of this book. In case you missed it, go ahead and take a peek—*it was student loan debt*. Believe me, I know exactly how overwhelming student loan debt can feel and be for college graduates. So I wanted to address the student loan debt crisis looming in our country head-on.

As a new college graduate entering the workforce, it's a great responsibility to carry tens and thousands of student loan debt with you. Some people feel trapped in the rat race of life when they have a big student loan payment hanging over their heads for the next ten years. Yet this is the brutal reality for many college graduates today.

I graduated from college in 1995. An American Council of Education (ACE) report shows the following student loan debt statistics for that year:[5]

- 48.7% of public four-year college graduates earning a Bachelor's degree had an average of $10,422 in federal student loan debt

---

5 "Federal Student Loan Debt: 1993 to 2004." American Council on Education. Accessed November 24, 2019. https://www.acenet.edu/news-room/Documents/IssueBrief-2005-Federal-Student-Loan-Debt-1993-to-2004.pdf.

- 51.5% private not-for-profit four-year college graduates earning a Bachelor's degree had an average of $14,250 in federal student loan debt

Source: U.S. Department of Education, National Center for Education Statistics. National Postsecondary Student Aid Studies: 1992–93, 1995–96, 1999–2000, and 2003–04.

I had $29,226 in federal student loan debt. And my mom's PLUS loan added another $8,000 on top of that to help cover my education expenses. Let's put this into perspective using the U.S. Department of Education's statistics. In comparison, I had more than twice the amount of student loan debt than other college graduates from private, not-for-profit four-year schools did.

How about the student loan debt statistics today? According to The Institute for College Access & Success, "Nationally, about two in three (65 percent) college seniors who graduated from public and private nonprofit colleges in 2018 had student loan debt. These borrowers owed an average of $29,200…"[6]

Just think I owed more than the average college graduate in 2018 back then. In 1995, I had a ridiculous amount of student loan debt. And with rising tuition expenses, students owe two to three times more these days. So trust me when I say this subject is near and dear to me.

---

6   "Student Debt and the Class of 2018." The Institute for College Access & Success. Accessed December 9, 2019. https://ticas. org/affordability-2/student-aid/student-debt-student-aid/ student-debt-and-the-class-of-2018/.

Honestly, I wanted to give student loan debt my utmost attention. That's why it took me so long to finish this book. It's all because I care that much about helping people with student loan debt. After all, we can't wait on Superman to solve the student loan debt problem in this country. It's up to each one of us to do our part.

STUDENT LOAN DEBT CAN BE CRIPPLING

> *"I make a six-figure salary and I still live paycheck-to-paycheck. At the rate I'm going, I'll probably die with my student loan debt. I've learned to stop worrying about it. Now I focus on helping my children avoid the same mistakes."*
> —Anonymous Student Loan Borrower

Millions of Americans are struggling with student loan debt. Graduating from college with a huge mountain of debt on your shoulders can be demoralizing. It can feel like you are about to take off in the biggest race of your life, only to find yourself held back with debt weight. Without the heavy burden of debt, you could run that race free as the wind.

People who are in deep feel the heavy weight student loan debt brings in their lives. Some of these people may feel stressed, embarrassed, and hopeless about the situation. An old proverb describes the eyes as "the window to the soul." I couldn't agree more. I have seen the pain in people's eyes when they open up to me about their student loan debt.

Before uttering a word about their student loan debt, they will either take a deep breath or make a sigh. That's how I usually know where the conversation is heading. Sometimes I may hear a little quiver in their voices, which remain relatively quiet at a whisper because it's that hard to talk about. On the other hand, if they are angry, those words flow out quickly like a river full of emotion.

As a matter of fact, a recent "Financial Taboos" survey conducted by The Harris Poll shows, "Student loan debt is the most uncomfortable financial topic to discuss..."[7] I believe it! I've seen it firsthand. Talking about student loan debt can get very emotional.

Student loan debt can put a financial strain on your life. It can also impact your relationships. For instance, the mere mention of student loans drove a wedge into my friend's marriage. She has a professional degree (e.g., M.D., J.D.) and six figures in student loan debt. And her husband refuses to pay one cent of it. He's adamant about her student loan debt being her full responsibility to pay back. His attitude is so atrocious about the topic that she has given up on discussing them with him to keep the peace. She finds the reality of this to be emotionally draining and damaging to their marriage.

There's no denying that student loan debt is changing our lives and the choices we make.

---

7   "Financial Taboos Survey." TD Ameritrade. Accessed November 25, 2019. https://s2.q4cdn.com/437609071/files/doc_news/research/2019/financial-taboos-survey.pdf.

Some people are so focused on paying off their student loan debt that they make tremendous sacrifices (career choices, retirement savings) to do it. These student loan borrowers make the tough decision of putting off marriage, starting a family, or buying a home (the American Dream) because they don't think it is possible. In other cases, people with big dreams may find themselves settling in life because they can't take on the "financial risk" to pursue them with student loan debt.

And I know this feeling all too well with my own career choice after school. I landed a job at a highly rated financial company. In the beginning, I was excited about the career opportunity ahead of me. The job was commission based with huge earnings potential. Commission only weighed heavily on my mind. After much thought and consideration, I quit in less than two weeks because I couldn't take the financial risk of a commission only job given my student loan payment obligation.

I was a little distraught about my student loan debt and job prospects after that decision. Somehow that big job I saw myself having after college—didn't come fast enough. In fact, I took jobs that didn't require any college education in the interim. So I wasn't making the kind of money I expected to earn with a college education.

Given this, I was very frustrated and decided to call my ex-boyfriend about it. While we hadn't dated since high school, he was someone I trusted. We had been friends since our middle school years. I talked to him about my disappointment and how I felt about everything. We had a meaningful conversation. In fact, it was very pivotal for me.

He listened to all of my concerns and gripes about life after college...student loans...jobs. I went on and on about my high student loan payments. He listened attentively to me. However, he had a different outlook on everything. Then he said in a serious and caring voice, "Kembala, God didn't bring you this far to leave you."

> *"Now faith is the substance of things hoped for,*
> *the evidence of things not seen."*
> —Hebrews 11:1 KJV

Those words gave me comfort. They enlightened and inspired me enough to change my outlook. And not long after our conversation, I landed my dream job at Andersen Consulting.

As student loan borrowers, we all have different experiences. A friend of mine recently told me she was absolutely disgusted about her student loan debt. Despite serving 20 years in the military, she didn't qualify for any student loan forgiveness because she did not make payments consistently for 10 years. She had a few periods of deferment and forbearance, which made her ineligible for the program. She said, "I can't see myself paying off all my student loans until I'm in my 70s. Do you hear me? That's 20 years from now." It's so disheartening to hear people lose hope about their student loan debt.

I'm a firm believer in the importance of *having hope*. And there is power in the words we speak. So I encourage you to speak words that will take you where you want to be. No matter how bad it looks right now, think positive and have a "can do" attitude. If you can change your mindset (like I talk about in Step #2), then you're more likely to see positive results follow.

WHAT YOU NEED TO KNOW ABOUT STUDENT LOAN DEBT

People consider student loan debt to be "good debt." They say it's "good debt" because it's an investment with low interest rates and you may receive tax benefits also. Besides you'll have more earning potential with a college degree.

Some borrowers view student loans as a means to an end. They think a student loan is the only way to close the expense gap of a high priced college education. When all else fails, student loans are the easy answer.

In hindsight, many student loan borrowers are frustrated because they never really understood what they were signing up for. Sure, they signed on the dotted line to get the money. But I highly doubt many students take the time to fully understand how student loans work, keep track of how much they are borrowing, or consider the future impact the debt will have on their lives. Otherwise, they may have made different decisions about acquiring student loan debt.

The reality of the matter is that most people typically get their first student loan at the age of 17 or 18 years old. This is too young to drink alcohol in the state of Florida. But at the stroke of a pen, you can start burying yourself into a mountain of student loan debt without any questions asked.

Since kids are signing the loans, some people blame the parents for the state of student loan debt in our country. Personally, I didn't call my mom for any approval on my student loans. She was a single mother and I didn't want to burden her with the discussion. Because we already decided the cost of a college education was worth the investment.

Speaking of investments, there are many investment vehicles like a 529 plan out there to help parents save for college. But some parents simply cannot afford to save for their children's college education. Whether they can afford to save or not, parents can still help their children with college planning.

It would be invaluable for parents to take an active role in talking to their children about the cost of a college education. Reviewing and comparing the financial aid packages is a great way to start the conversation. Ideally it's not a one and done matter. Being diligent about managing the cost of a college education together from start to finish should help kids graduate school with less debt.

Nevertheless there are parents who may not feel comfortable with their own financial understanding to provide their children with the necessary guidance on student loans. We know this to be true for educators who lack the confidence in teaching personal finance in school. In fact, a "University of Wisconsin study confirmed that more than 80% of teachers don't feel confident teaching personal finance."[8] And these are people who teach for a living.

---

8   Pelletier, John. "Not enough teachers know the basics of financial education," MarketWatch, April 29, 2019, https://www.marketwatch.com/story/not-enough-teachers-know-the-basics-of-financial-education-2019-04-18.

However, parents can still play an active role in helping their kids to minimize student loan debt. They can go to college planning and financial aid discussions held at local schools, libraries, churches, and other venues to help improve their knowledge and understanding. There's also a wealth of information available online on how to pay for college. Ideally, *students should seek out scholarships and grants to fund their education because they do not require repayment.*

HOW TO MINIMIZE STUDENT LOAN DEBT

1. **Fill out the Free Application for Federal Student Aid (FAFSA®) early**

The FAFSA is used to determine how much financial aid you can receive from the government (federal, state), schools, colleges, universities, and private resources to pay your educational expenses. Don't make the mistake of not filling out the FAFSA because you could be leaving tens of thousands of dollars on the table for your education. What's the FAFSA? According to StudentAid.gov:[9]

> The FAFSA form asks a series of questions that determine whether you are a dependent or independent student for purposes of applying for federal student aid. If you are a dependent student, you must report parent information, as well as your own information, on your application.

When you complete your FAFSA on-time, you may receive financial aid offers from schools. For example, you could

---

9 "Filling Out the FAFSA® Form." Federal Student Aid. Accessed December 9, 2019. https://studentaid.ed.gov/sa/fafsa/filling-out.

receive scholarships, grants, low-interest student loans, and work-study programs.

IMPORTANT NOTE: You have a better shot at receiving more financial aid when you fill out your FAFSA earlier because some states and schools have limited funds available to give students. In other words, if you fill it out late, you may qualify for less money because it's already been given to other students. Some states and schools actually distribute financial aid money on a "first come, first served" basis.

2. Make Financials a Part of Your School Selection Criteria Upfront

We all use different criteria to evaluate schools. There are a variety of things to consider: location, academic needs, accreditation, school size, ranking, and more. The *total cost of your education* cannot be forgotten.

Sometimes the excitement of getting into your dream school makes it easy to overlook the cost. Be sure to factor in the education cost into your school selection process. Questions to consider:

How much is tuition? Will you be living on campus? What are your expenses? Do you have any scholarships or grants to help reduce the costs? What type of financial aid package are you being offered?

Review your prospective school's "Cost of Attendance" to see the estimated cost for attendance. The Cost of Attendance (COA) gives you an overview of the expected costs and expenses at a specific school for a year. The U.S. Department of Education states:[10]

> The cost of attendance (COA) is not the bill that you may get from your college; it is the total amount it will cost you to go to college each year. The COA includes tuition and fees; on-campus room and board (or a housing and food allowance for off-campus students); and allowances for books, supplies, transportation, loan fees, and, if applicable, dependent care. It can also include other expenses like an allowance for the rental or purchase of a personal computer, costs related to a disability, or costs for eligible study-abroad programs.

U.S. News reported, "The average cost of tuition and fees for the 2018–2019 school year was $35,676 at private colleges, $9,716 for state residents at public colleges and $21,629 for out-of-state students at state schools."[11]

As you can see, private college tuition is usually the most expensive. This reminds me of the time when my University of Miami (UM) business school professor posed one of the most thought-provoking questions to our class. He stood silently in front of the class with his arms folded and looked

---

10 "Cost of Attendance." U.S. Department of Education. Accessed December 10, 2019. https://fafsa.ed.gov/help/costatt.htm.
11 Powell, Farran and Emma Kerr. "What You Need to Know About College Tuition Costs." U.S. News & World Report. September 18, 2019. https://www.usnews.com/education/best-colleges/paying-for-college/articles/what-you-need-to-know-about-college-tuition-costs.

very intently at each one of us. Then in a direct and serious, yet curious tone the professor asked:

"Why are you going here instead of Florida International University (FIU) where you could pay much less?"

I could not believe my ears. For additional context, I went to school in-state. UM is a private university. And FIU is a public university nearby.

The class was shocked and sat quietly in disbelief. The question made you want to scratch your head and think about it. Perhaps that's what some people did because everyone was speechless and blown away.

Our professor seemed to welcome the deafening silence. After all, teachers love an attentive audience—don't they?

Then he proceeded to talk about some of the other differences between the two universities besides *the cost*. Our class discussion was a memorable one. And it didn't change my decision about going to UM; I went on to graduate later.

When it comes to your education, the choice is yours. Parents can be instrumental in helping you make the right decision. I've seen parents who work very hard to help their children minimize student loan debt, who still factor in more than the cost into that decision. For example, some of their selection criteria may include: school accreditation, location, reputation, majors available, cost, student/teacher ratio, and profit/not-for-profit.

I've talked with money savvy parents who encourage their kids to go to community college for the first two years and stay at home to keep costs low. A study showed students who take this route usually perform better in the classroom and make wiser financial decisions. It's okay to go a different route than your classmates who may take the plunge to go straight to a high-priced, big name major university across the country instead.

Of course, public in-state tuition is usually much lower than out-of-state. And private is typically more expensive than public. Cost conscious parents help their children understand the school expenses and try to steer them in a favorable direction. Take a close look at those financial aid packages because some prestigious colleges and universities may offer you a very attractive one. For example, a friend of mine said it cost him less money to send his child out-of-state to Princeton University than to an in-state public university.

3. "Begin with the End in Mind"

Studies show college graduates tend to earn $1,000,000 more than those without a college education over a lifetime. But that doesn't mean that everyone needs a college education to be successful.

Many professions do not require a formal college education. For example, some jobs may only require a trade school and/or apprenticeship. If you are having a hard time figuring out what you want to do, a personality test (e.g., Myers-Briggs) could be useful in providing some career guidance.

Ideally, you want to think about your educational objective before you start college or obtain a student loan. Being intentional about your actions will help you to make smarter decisions and save more money.

Questions to consider: What do you want to be (education needs, career path, earning potential)? How much student loan debt are you willing to take out? When will you pay it back? Have you explored scholarships, grants, employer tuition assistance programs, and other ways to reduce your education expenses?

No matter what field you choose, it's important to improve your knowledge. Reading books, attending seminars and workshops, and continuing to build your knowledge (online, video tutorials) will help you grow. As Jim Rohn once said, "Formal education will make you a living; self-education will make you a fortune."

Speaking of fortunes, Warren Buffett is highly regarded as one of the most successful investors in the world. He offered a group of high school students at The Nebraska Forum for Nebraska Students some great words of wisdom on college debt. Check out the video "How to Stay Out of Debt: Warren Buffett—Financial Future of American Youth (1999)" on YouTube to hear Buffett's thoughts on debt—https://www.youtube.com/watch?v=IvveZr0D_9Y.

4. Know Before You Owe

Ignorance is not bliss. Some people struggling with student loan debt regret not having had a better understanding of how student loans worked. They never really understood the terms of their loans before they signed on the dotted line. And many people say they never considered the impact student loan debt would have on their lives after school.

If knowledge is power, a lack of it can make you feel like a weakling.

> *"If you think you won't be able to pay off the debt after graduation, don't take out a loan. If you do take out a student loan, pay it off. Be an adult about it."*
> - Anonymous, "Student Loan Debt in America" survey

We need to make informed decisions about acquiring student loan debt. It's worth your time to educate yourself about student loans (types, restrictions, repayment process) beforehand. There are so many loan options available—it can be confusing.

I remember when I had to make a quick decision about two different types of Stafford student loans. I took the forms and asked the financial aid representative, "What is the difference between these two loans"? She was mum. I only received a blank, glassy-eyed stare in response to the question as she waited for me to fill one out.

Back in those days, to be truly informed I would have had to sit down and read each loan agreement thoroughly. But I didn't take the time to do it. Fortunately, it wasn't a big loan because I made the wrong decision. I selected the unsubsidized loan, which we'll get into momentarily.

Looking back it was a huge mistake to make such a rash and uninformed decision. I had two choices and I clearly remember them, a Subsidized or Unsubsidized Stafford loan. And I picked the unsubsidized one. Ugggh! Perhaps this happened to me, so that I could share this story with you.

For those who are unfamiliar with *the difference between subsidized and unsubsidized loans,* the biggest difference is who pays the interest (the cost) hence the word "subsidized." StudentAid.Ed.gov highlights this key difference:[12]

The U.S. Department of Education pays the interest on a Direct Subsidized Loan

- while you're in school at least half-time,
- for the first six months after you leave school (referred to as a grace period*), and
- during a period of deferment (a postponement of loan payments).

Direct Unsubsidized Loans:

- You are responsible for paying the interest on a Direct Unsubsidized Loan during all periods.
- If you choose not to pay the interest while you are in school and during grace periods and deferment or forbearance periods, your interest will accrue (accumulate) and be capitalized (that is, your interest will be added to the principal amount of your loan).

Source: StudentAid.gov

---

12 "Subsidized and Unsubsidized Loans." Federal Student Aid. Accessed November 24, 2019. https://studentaid.ed.gov/sa/types/loans/subsidized-unsubsidized.

Since I chose the unsubsidized student loan the government did not pay the interest while I was in school. So I was responsible for the interest at all times. I didn't pay any interest on my loans during school, so the balance on this one increased.

A lot has changed since I went to college. And I'm not just talking about all of the cool back-to-school dorm swag that never existed back then. Now student loan borrowers must receive entrance counseling before they take out a federal direct subsidized and unsubsidized loan. The primary goal of the entrance counseling is to help ensure you understand your responsibilities and obligations as a student loan borrower. For more on entrance counseling, please visit studentloans.gov.

Students also have the luxury of having a wealth of information on student loans available online at the click of a button. Take advantage of these resources to help you make better decisions about student loans upfront.

5. Not All Student Loans are Created Equal

Generally, there are two types of student loans—federal and private. The U.S. government funds federal student loans. Private student loans are not federally backed. Financial institutions like banks or credit unions, schools and other organizations (e.g., state agency) fund private student loans.

Federal student loans are often cheaper than private student loans. They typically offer you a lower fixed interest rate. Federal student loans also give you more benefits like subsidized interest payments, income based repayment plans, student loan forgiveness programs, and more flexibility to repay your loans.

"Private student loans should be avoided at all costs."
—Suze Orman

A PLUS loan is a federally backed student loan available for parents. This student loan helps parents to fund their dependent child's education. While the child benefits from the PLUS student loan funds, the parent is the one legally responsible for repaying the student loan.

According to StudentAid.gov to be eligible to receive a parent PLUS loan you must:[13]

- be the biological or adoptive parent (or in some cases, the stepparent) of a dependent undergraduate student enrolled at least half-time at an eligible school;
- not have an adverse credit history (unless you meet certain additional requirements); and
- meet the general eligibility requirements for federal student aid. (Your child must also meet these requirements.)

  Note: Grandparents (unless they have legally adopted the dependent student) and legal guardians are not eligible to receive parent PLUS loans, even if they have had primary responsibility for raising the student.

---

13 "PLUS Loans." Federal Student Aid. Accessed on November 24, 2019. https://studentaid.ed.gov/sa/types/loans/plus.

Professional and graduate students may also take advantage of PLUS federal student loans. Studentaid.ed.gov defines the PLUS student loan as follows:

> The U.S. Department of Education makes Direct PLUS Loans to eligible parents and graduate or professional students through schools participating in the Direct Loan Program.
>
> Note: A Direct PLUS Loan is commonly referred to as a parent PLUS loan when made to a parent, and as a grad PLUS loan when made to a graduate or professional student.
>
> Here's a quick overview of Direct PLUS Loans:
>
> - The U.S. Department of Education is your lender.
> - You must not have an adverse credit history. A credit check will be conducted. If you have an adverse credit history, you may still be able to receive a PLUS loan if you meet additional requirements.
> - The maximum PLUS loan amount you can receive is the cost of attendance (determined by the school) minus any other financial aid received.
>
> Source: StudentAid.gov, visit studentaid.gov for more information

There is a stark difference between federal and private student loans. Most private loans require you to have a credit check and/or cosigner. Before you sign off on a loan make sure you review and understand the credit terms (e.g., prepayment penalty, variable/fixed interest rate). For example, you need to know if your lender requires you to make interest payments during school.

HOW TO PAY OFF STUDENT LOAN DEBT

"I had three jobs in college. The best day of my life was when I paid off my student loans, on my own."
—Jessica Seinfeld

The approach for paying off student loan debt is like any other debt. In fact, I used the same techniques in this book to pay off all of my student loan debt (including my mom's PLUS loan) three years early. Sure, I could have paid them off even earlier had I been laser-sharp focused on doing so, but you have to *live*. And I have no regrets about the decisions I made.

While I made paying off my student loan debt a top priority after graduation, it wasn't the only one. I worked to build up savings (emergency, general, retirement) for the future. I also invested some money (employee stock purchase plan). These actions helped to give me more financial security. And I was able to achieve other personal goals too. For example, I paid cash for my beautiful wedding and we put a 20% down payment on our first home.

When I say we, I am talking about my husband and me. We both graduated from the University of Miami with student loan debt. And we still had our student loans when we got married. Thankfully, we had a serious money conversation before we said, "I do." In fact, I saw his credit report and we talked about our personal finances together.

After we got married, we initially took a separate his and hers approach to paying off our student loans. In other words, he paid his and I paid mine. Given our strong determination to pay them off early, we each paid extra every month.

When I got pregnant with our first child, I had an "Aha!" moment. It was to become debt-free (except for our mortgage). My personal debt consisted of several student loans and an auto loan, which amounted to a little over $20,000 in total. So I created my debt-free action plan to make it happen.

My husband and I discussed my goal. He gave me a lot of moral support to achieve it, but I paid off all my debt on my own less than seven months later. And I think the biggest thrill I had doing it was seeing those balances drop lower and lower. It was also nice to receive my car title in the mail. Yes!!!

A year or so later, we wrote a big check to pay off his student loan debt. It was the best feeling ever to be able to write that check! I didn't think of it as his or mine. We were happy to do it together. Fortunately, we paid off our student loan debt early and we didn't have any more in our house. It was finally gone!

There are many people who have managed to pay off significant student loan debt. We may have our own journeys, but we all take it one payment at a time. For example, someone might work multiple jobs, make big sacrifices (live very frugally), minimize expenses (avoid major purchases), and put major life changes on hold with one goal in mind—to pay off student loan debt.

We all make different choices in life. What works for Sally may not work for Joe. It's not how they do it, but the fact that people are getting out of student loan debt that matters most. Yes, it's possible. If we can do it, then so can you!

> *"Prioritize paying it off. Just because the rates*
> *seem low on a nominal basis doesn't mean the*
> *interest doesn't add up to you paying massive*
> *amounts more at the end."*
> —Anonymous, "Student Loan Debt in America" survey

Take it One Payment at a Time…

If you can commit to the payment schedule they lay out for you, you should pay off your student loan debt right on time—normally within 10 years.

Keep in mind student loans accrue interest, so it's best to pay them off sooner rather than later because it costs you less money. Plus, you can't beat the peace of mind and freedom you'll have once it's finally paid off! Paying off your student loan debt is a big deal worth singing, screaming, and shouting about doing.

WHAT IF YOU CAN'T AFFORD THE PAYMENTS?

Paying off my student loans wasn't easy, especially given some periods of unemployment and underemployment after school. There was a time when I felt very uncomfortable about being able to afford my student loan payments with all of my other living expenses. And I picked up the phone and talked with my lenders about my concerns. They discussed some options available for me—deferment or forbearance.

FederalStudentAid defines deferment and forbearance as follows:[14]

What are deferment and forbearance?

If you meet certain eligibility requirements, deferment or forbearance allows you to temporarily stop making payments or to temporarily reduce your monthly payment amount for a specified period.

What's the difference between deferment and forbearance?

The main difference is that with a deferment, you may not be responsible for paying the interest that accrues on certain types of loans during the deferment period.

I qualified to defer my student loans, so I didn't have to make any student loan payments for a specific period of time. This helped alleviate some of the financial pressure I felt. However, I did not want my student loan balances to balloon and I managed to pay them anyway. I made some personal sacrifices to do this. For example, I moved back home with my mom and later with my Aunt Ginny to minimize my living expenses. Thankfully, I had these options available 22 months after college.

---

14 "Deferment and Forbearance." Federal Student Aid. Accessed on November 24, 2019. https://studentaid.ed.gov/sa/repay-loans/deferment-forbearance.

BIGGEST STUDENT LOAN MISTAKES TO AVOID

1. **Believing You Don't Have to Pay Them Back If You Don't Graduate**

    "I got one thing out of college: bad credit. That was all I got— some student loans, man. I didn't know they wanted you to pay that back. I thought that was only if you graduated."
    —Kevin Bozeman

Some people think if they don't finish school, they don't have to pay their student loans back. That's not true. You signed a promissory note that you would pay the money back according to specified terms.

So take that agreement seriously and read it. After all, it's legally binding.

2. **Avoiding Lenders and Ignoring Bills When You Can't Pay**

    "I'm speaking on behalf of all the people who ever took out a student loan for college when I say, 'Back up off me, Citibank! Back up! Because I know I'm late on my payments, but stop calling me, and stop shouting at me in those nasty letters,'"
    —Finesse Mitchell

If you cannot afford to make your student loan payments as agreed, contact your lender now. Depending on your financial situation, your lender may have more affordable payment options available to assist you. For example, you may qualify for a program that lowers your monthly payments or defers them.

An income-driven repayment plan may be your best option for federal student loans. This sets your monthly payment amount based on your income. Visit StudentAid.gov for federal (government) loans to learn more about programs available to help you.

> **IMPORTANT NOTE: Please note these special government repayment programs are FREE to enroll in, so don't waste your hard-earned money paying any third party (i.e. Student Loan Debt Relief company) to help you enroll or apply for these types of programs. Do it yourself and save.**

Student Aid.gov defines income-driven repayment plans as follows:[15]

An income-driven repayment plan sets your monthly student loan payment at an amount that is intended to be affordable based on your income and family size. We offer four income-driven repayment plans:

- Revised Pay As You Earn Repayment Plan (REPAYE Plan)
- Pay As You Earn Repayment Plan (PAYE Plan)

---

15 "Income-Driven Plans." Federal Student Aid. Accessed on November 24, 2019. https://studentaid.ed.gov/sa/repay-loans/understand/plans/income-driven.

- Income-Based Repayment Plan (IBR Plan)
- Income-Contingent Repayment Plan (ICR Plan)

Source: StudentAid.gov — Income Repayment Plans

3. Consolidating Student Loans When You Really Shouldn't

"Seeing the light of day. Especially, when I mistakenly consolidated some of my loans."
- Anonymous, "Student Loan Debt in America" survey

You have to consider the pros and cons carefully before you consolidate your student loan debt. What's the interest rate? How much will it cost you? What's the repayment period? Compare the new terms (payment amount, benefits) against the old to help ensure you make the right decision.

Student loan consolidation may be a good option for people who want to have a single payment or lower payments overall. **Key word being "may" because you have to be careful with student loan consolidation.** It could be bad when you consolidate your loans at a higher fixed interest rate just to have one single payment.

For example, I knew someone who consolidated all his student loans at a fixed interest rate of 9.0%. Before he did the consolidation, some of his loans only had a 5% interest rate. After he consolidated, his student loan repayment schedule also reset. In other words, he had to start over with a new 10-year repayment schedule. Not to mention, the principal balance now included all of the interest from every loan consolidated. As a result, student loan consolidation cost him more money in interest.

It could get downright ugly when you consolidate your federal and private student loans together. Some people consider this option to save more money (payments, interest). However, when you consolidate your federal and private student loans together, you lose all of your federal loan benefits (income-based repayment, student loan forgiveness, deferment).

> *"...Everyone says consolidate but before you do be careful and do the math to make sure you will pay less than if you keep them separate. Further, make sure all of the other conditions are agreeable with you. Also ensure you have provisions that allow you to suspend payments temporarily in case of adverse life event."*
> —Anonymous, "Student Loan Debt in America" survey

4. Defaulting on Your Student Loans

> *"Stay current and make sure if you can't make the payments, reach out and ask for deferral or other payment arrangements."*
> - Anonymous, "Student Loan Debt in America" survey

A student loan default is the worst thing that you could let happen. You default on your student loan when you fail to make payments on the loan and let them get delinquent. For example, some lenders may consider your loan in default when you don't make a payment for 240 days. Keep in mind that the period of time required to default on student loans varies.

If you can't afford to make your student loan payments, contact your lender immediately to discuss your financial situation. Your lender may have payment options available to help you avoid default. For example, lenders may lower your payments or temporarily defer payments.

5 Reasons to Avoid Student Loan Default:

1. **You Could Ruin Your Credit Score**. Student loans are reported to the credit reporting companies. If you don't pay on time, it will negatively impact your credit score.
2. **Your Wages Could Be Garnished**. Your employer may be required to take a portion of your paycheck for student loan repayment.
3. **You Could Lose Your Tax Refund.** The IRS can take any federal and some state tax refunds until you've paid off your student loans.
4. **Your Federal Benefits Could Be Reduced**. The government may reduce the amount of federal benefits you receive (up to 15%) for student loans. For example, Social Security recipients may have a portion of their monthly benefits reduced to repay student loan debt.
5. **You Could Get Sued**. Lenders have the ability to sue you to collect for student loan debt owed. Remember the promissory note is a legally binding agreement.

There are more consequences for student loan default. According to Federal Student Aid:[16]

- The entire unpaid balance of your loan and any interest you owe becomes immediately due (this is called "acceleration").
- You can no longer receive deferment or forbearance, and you lose eligibility for other benefits, such as the ability to choose a repayment plan.
- You will lose eligibility for additional federal student aid.
- The default will be reported to credit bureaus, damaging your credit rating and affecting your ability to buy a car or house or to get a credit card.
- Your tax refunds and federal benefit payments may be withheld and applied toward repayment of your defaulted loan (this is called "Treasury offset").
- Your wages will be garnished. This means your employer may be required to withhold a portion of your pay and send it to your loan holder to repay your defaulted loan.
- Your loan holder can take you to court.
- You may not be able to purchase or sell assets such as real estate.
- You may be charged court costs, collection fees, attorney's fees, and other costs associated with the collection process.
- It may take years to reestablish a good credit record.

---

16 "What are the consequences of default?" Federal Student Aid. Accessed on November 24, 2019. https://studentaid.ed.gov/sa/repay-loans/default#consequences.

- Your school may withhold your academic transcript until your defaulted student loan is satisfied. The academic transcript is the property of the school, and it is the school's decision—not the U.S. Department of Education's or your loan holder's—whether to release the transcript to you.

Source: StudentAid.gov, please visit their site for more information about the consequences of defaulting on your student loan.

HOW TO REBOUND AFTER STUDENT LOAN DEFAULT

ONE DAY I RECEIVED a call from someone who really needed my help with her finances. We'll call her Gloria. When I spoke to Gloria, I could sense the urgency and hear the despair in her voice. She told me her income tax refund was being held captive.

You know that *big check* that some people can't wait to get in tax season? The one they've already accounted for on how to spend every dollar. Yes, that's the check.

Gloria was expecting a $10,000 check from the IRS. When she didn't receive her tax refund check on time, she called her tax preparer. They both verified the tax return and routing number information—everything looked good. So Gloria decided to wait a little longer. After some time, Gloria called the IRS to get the status of her tax refund. That's when she heard a recording regarding her tax refund status, "The check in the amount of $10,000 was intercepted by the Student Loan..."

Gloria was shocked! She finally understood what happened to her check. Gloria called her lender and found out her student loan was in default. There was nothing she could do about that IRS check. It was gone. The money went to pay her student loan debt.

How would you feel if this happened to you? It's a real dilemma.

Gloria did not even know that she had defaulted on her student loan. And she certainly did not know the government could take your IRS tax refund when you do. Remember as you just read earlier, when you default "tax refunds and federal benefit payments may be withheld and applied toward repayment of your defaulted loan (this is called 'Treasury offset')." Yes, it really happens.

Sadly, there was nothing Gloria could do about that check. Not receiving that money only put her further behind. This situation left Gloria in a serious bind financially and emotionally.

At this point we could only move forward. So we talked about how she got there and the options she had on the table to resolve the situation. Over the next few months, I worked with Gloria using a holistic approach to help her get her finances back on track. We started with the basics looking at the money she had coming in and going out.

Then, we created a budget and a plan to pay down debt. She made some tough decisions to reduce her expenses and was committed to paying off her debt. Gloria put in the work and made tremendous progress to achieve her goals.

As a result of her efforts she completely satisfied her lender's student loan rehabilitation program requirements. Yes! Gloria's student loan was taken out of default.

When you default on your student loan there are usually several options available to get out of default:

- Pay in Full (I know, who would ever default if they could afford the payments—right?)
- Loan Rehabilitation
- Consolidate the Loan

If your student loan is in default, contact your lender to understand what options are available to get it out of default. In Gloria's case a loan rehabilitation program worked perfectly to get her loan out of default. She worked with her lender to get more affordable monthly payments too.

5. Don't Keep Putting Your Student Loans Off and Deferring Interest Payments

> *"Students should start to pay back their loan as soon as they get a job upon graduating. Do not take advantage of the deferred payments or forbearance as the interest adds up quickly. Also, go to school for what you want instead and try not to change careers as additional degrees can add up to more debt."*
> - Anonymous, "Student Loan Debt in America" survey

Sometimes people do not want to face their student loan debt, so they keep putting them off. In some instances, they will stay in school to avoid the payments. These "professional students" earn a lot of degrees to avoid paying their student loan debt. This can be a HUGE and costly mistake! Yes, you're in school and have a valid reason to defer your payments.

But your student loan debt isn't going anywhere. It just keeps growing and growing.

It's best to start paying your student loan debt off as soon as possible. Deferring your student loan debt and pursuing more levels of education could cost you big time. I read about a married couple pursuing their education goals, which resulted in over $700,000 in student loan debt for them. For real! They are in deep.

6.   Not Applying for Student Loan Forgiveness

"Depending on where you work, you may qualify
for loan forgiveness. Do your research to
try to eliminate this debt."
- Anonymous, "Student Loan Debt in America" survey

Not applying for student loan forgiveness programs when you qualify is an unfortunate mistake. You may be able to receive student loan forgiveness based on your job. For example, teachers and people who work in public service may qualify to have their student loans forgiven.

Student loans may be discharged for other reasons also, such as disability or school closures. Visit StudentAid.gov to find out more about the criteria to get your student loan forgiven, cancelled, or discharged. You can also find out information on how to apply for student loan forgiveness.

STUDENT LOAN DEBT IN AMERICA—SURVEY SAYS...

"Where there's a will, there's a way."

First, I'd like to send a BIG THANK YOU to the hundreds of people who responded to my "Student Loan Debt in America" survey. I really appreciate your candor and the time you spent sharing your personal experiences (challenges, tips) with me. It was very helpful in giving me more insight into how student loan debt is touching real people's lives.

I know talking about student loan debt is not an easy topic. It can be quite emotional, especially when your debt balloons and you see absolutely no way out because you simply cannot afford it. Or you may have a little resentment about the debt because you think your school failed you. Perhaps that degree you worked so hard to earn just isn't paying off (higher income) the way you thought it would. I hear you loud and clearly.

This survey also confirmed people have different journeys. Some people had minimal student loan debt and experienced little to no challenges paying it back and moving on. On the other hand, some borrowers had to work extremely hard (sometimes multiple jobs) and make tremendous sacrifices to pay them off. Unfortunately, many people experienced financial challenges for a variety of reasons (health, unemployment, household expenses), which resulted in them carrying the heavy burden of student loan debt past the normal 10-year repayment period.

Most people agree student loan debt is a necessary investment to have a better shot at life. Figure 1 shows how much student loan debt survey respondents have owed:

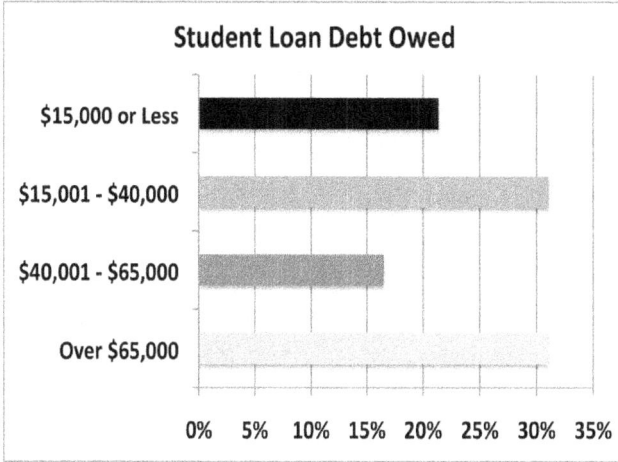

Figure 1

The following are additional data insights from the "Student Loan Debt in America" survey respondents:

- 89% graduated; 11% did not graduate.
- 60% still have student loan debt; 40% paid off all of their student loan debt.
- People who paid off all their student loans: 57% early, 16% on-time, 27% late.
- 61% had student loan debt over 11 years.

You have to take action on your student loans to eliminate them. Here are some helpful tips to manage your student loan debt from survey respondents:

- Live within your means and don't go into credit card debt. Create a budget and minimize your expenses, so that you can pay more than the minimum student loan payment. Don't waste your money paying interest.
- Consistently pay on your student loans, so they don't go into default. Never give up!
- Consider joining the military. The GI bill pays for college, including earning a master's degree.
- Set up a payment plan for your student loan debt. Contact the lender if you can't afford to pay. They will probably work with you.
- Try to double up on your payment or put a little extra to pay off the loan faster. Check out www.fastweb.com before you take out any more student loans.
- Consider consolidating your student loans or negotiating more affordable payments.
- Move back home with your parents, so you can pay down the principal. I would highly recommend living at home for one to two years. It's not as bad as it sounds.
- If you join the military, pay the interest while you are on active duty. This will allow you to have significant reductions in your overall student loan debt.
- Pay off your student loans as quickly as possible. You'll be better off.
- Make paying off your student loans a priority. You signed a contractual agreement; so make sure you include the student loan payment in your budget. Try to pay it off early and pay more on the principal. Paying off the loans helps your credit score. Avoid frivolous spending or any

costly leisure activities. To minimize your expenses: stay at home and don't make big purchases (jewelry, expensive cars, pricey vacations, house). Be more frugal with your spending habits like clothing and eating out.

- Don't take out more student loans than you actually need. And don't use the money for "non-school" things.
- Make the necessary sacrifices to pay your student loan on-time, so it won't negatively impact your credit.
- Student loan debt can be a beast. The first thing is you have to be COMMITTED to getting rid of it. This means, if you can afford it, paying more than the monthly payment. You may have to forgo some luxury personal items for yourself. Each time you reduce your total balance by 10%, celebrate the accomplishment with something inexpensive you really like. Also ask yourself, can you afford to increase your monthly payment after reaching this milestone? If you can, now make payments with the new amount. This will speed up the repayment even faster. In the end, it'll be worth it.
- Don't overborrow! Too much student loan debt can feel like a black cloud hanging over you for many years to come.
- Pay interest in school and during any forbearance or deferment periods. This will help you to minimize your student loan debt.
- When you have more money, use it to pay more on your student loan debt. Focus on paying down the principal.
- Select career opportunities that allow you to pay your student loan debt.

- Pay off any high interest rate debt (e.g., credit card) first because your student loans usually have lower interest.

The major challenge people face paying off their student loans is having the money to do so. Many people feel they do not earn enough income to pay their student loan debt along with "everything else." For example, some people earning what is perceived to be a "high salary" still had problems affording their high student loan payments given their other household expenses (housing, childcare, transportation, healthcare). This is especially true for those borrowers who have experienced periods of underemployment and unemployment.

However, some people do not prioritize their student loan debt. They can't seem to fit it into their budgets. So it often gets overlooked. One person expressed the amount owed felt so "insurmountable" that it was easy to disregard making payments and just spend money elsewhere.

Several people felt overwhelmed and hopeless about their student loans because:

- The balances grew during deferments.
- They were being charged too much interest.
- They didn't finish school or thought the degree was not worth the price.
- They had problems keeping up because the payments were too high.

On the flip side, 15% of survey respondents didn't experience any challenges paying their student loans. Here are some of the reasons why:

- I only had a small amount of student loan debt. And I made all of my payments on time. Later, I used a home equity line of credit to pay them off.
- My parents paid for undergraduate school. During graduate school, they gave me an interest-free loan. I also earned a working scholarship, which cut my tuition expenses in half. After graduation, I paid my parents back $200/month until the loan was finally paid off.
- I had minimal student loan debt. I planned ahead to account for making my student loan payments. To keep expenses down, I rented a sensibly priced apartment and bought a used car.
- I went to school in the 1970s and I got a low interest loan through my parent's job. I worked two jobs during college to make my student loan payments. After school, I "got a good job" and in a couple of years I paid the loan back. Keep in mind tuition was much less expensive back then.

In hindsight, some survey respondents offered this advice:

- Take advantage of free schools.
- Do not take out any interest based student loans. Pay cash for school. If you can't afford it, select a trade or apprenticeship.
- Pick an affordable undergraduate school. Do not obtain a graduate degree unless you have a plan for how doing so will increase your earnings. Make sure to take into consideration the industry you will be working in.
- Take advantage of any employer tuition assistance programs.
- Avoid student loan debt.

- Don't miss your student loan payments.
- Do your best. Be sure to work with your loan provider if you can't make the payments.
- Don't go to expensive schools. Consider the earning potential of the degree. Also don't go to college just because everyone thinks you should. There are a lot of opportunities out there that don't require a college education.
- Save money with generational family living.
- Consider the impact student loan debt will have on your life. It is an added expense that you have to include every month. Student loan forgiveness payments can be high and seem like forever to get any relief.
- Go to a community college or more affordable school for the first two years. Then transfer to a big school to finish. That way you receive the same degree at only half the price.
- Grab the free money!!! Do your research on scholarships and grants. Use the Internet to find out about more. Avoid taking out extra money in student loans because the interest adds up quickly.
- Beware of student loan consolidation because it may make you ineligible for government repayment plans (income based repayment).
- Minimize your student loan debt. Pay 30% more than your student loan payment every month.
- Try to avoid taking out any student loans. Borrow from your family members to get cheaper rates and more favorable terms. If this is not possible, get federal student loans only.

There are millions of people with student loan debt in America. My survey confirmed the sacrifices (retirement savings, homeownership) many people have made to pay off their student loan debt. And the real struggles people young and old have with paying their student loan debt despite working one or more jobs. For some people student loan debt has had a negative impact on their mental health, self-worth, credit score, and/or relationships.

FINAL THOUGHTS

In closing, as you can see everyone has an opinion on student loan debt. And personal finance experts are no different. They often warn students and parents alike to avoid taking on student loan debt, especially when you can't afford to pay it back. These experts advise you to save for college and/or work and pay cash instead.

Some personal finance experts, myself included, view student loans as an investment in yourself. We understand the need for student loans to pursue a higher education. However, you must be prudent about this decision. A good rule to follow to help you minimize the burden is to make sure the total amount borrowed is less than you'll earn in your first year's salary. And you must be diligent about paying it off as soon as possible.

If you're in student loan debt already, I can tell you there is light at the end of the tunnel. Reading this book alone won't get you there. But I truly believe if you apply the principles you've learned in this book and pair it with your sheer determination to succeed, you'll pay them off.

> *"To be successful in life, you must get in the habit of turning negatives into positives."*
> —George Foreman

DEBT SETTLEMENT

READ THIS BEFORE YOU SETTLE ANY DEBT

Are you thinking about settling your debt? It's best to follow through on your commitment to pay your creditor in full. However, if extenuating circumstances prevent you from paying your account as agreed and you're thinking about settling your debt, then here's what you need to know *before settling*:

- **Do it yourself and avoid paying a debt settlement company to do it for you.**
- **Negotiate a repayment plan with your creditor before it goes to collections.** Creditors are usually easier to work with than debt collection agencies, so contact your creditor to discuss a repayment plan that works for you. Be up front about any circumstances that are preventing you (e.g., unemployment) from paying as agreed.
- **Settling your account may negatively impact your credit report.** If your creditor agrees to accept less than the amount owed, it could be reported as settled and affect your credit score.

- **The IRS may treat any reduced debt as taxable income.** This means you could owe taxes on the amount of debt you were forgiven. Talk with a tax expert or visit irs.gov for the latest information on IRS rules and regulations.
- **Beware of creditors who ask for electronic access to your financial institution's account to settle.** Typically, creditors settle for an upfront lump sum cash amount only. For example, you may pay $400 (50–60% off) in cash on an outstanding balance of $900. In the event they agree to a payment plan and request electronic access to your account for withdrawals, *don't give it to them*. If you allow them to automatically withdraw money from your account, you no longer have control of when or how much you pay them unless you close the account.
- **Always get the settlement agreement (full terms) in writing before you settle your debt.** Any agreement that you make should be received in writing to ensure your creditor's commitment to the terms of your settlement.

WHAT YOU NEED TO KNOW ABOUT DEBT SETTLEMENT COMPANIES

Are you tired of hearing those debt relief commercials that sound too good to be true? They tout irresistible offers *to wipe away your debt fast and easy*. In some cases, they even proclaim the government will pay your debt with bailout money. Sadly, some debt settlement companies leave customers with empty promises, no debt relief, and in some cases, worse off than before.

The **Federal Trade Commission (FTC)** "deals with issues that touch the economic life of every American. The FTC is the only federal agency with both consumer protection and competition jurisdiction in broad sectors of the economy."[17] It offers consumers the guidance below on debt settlement and debt relief companies:

> Debt settlement programs typically are offered by for-profit companies, and involve the company negotiating with your creditors to allow you to pay a "settlement" to resolve your debt. The settlement is another word for a lump sum that's less than the full amount you owe. To make that lump sum payment, the program asks that you set aside a specific amount of money every month in savings. Debt settlement companies usually ask that you transfer this amount every month into an escrow-like account to accumulate enough savings to pay off a settlement that is reached eventually. Further, these programs often encourage or instruct their clients to stop making any monthly payments to their creditors.

> **Debt Settlement Has Risks**

> Although a debt settlement company may be able to settle one or more of your debts, consider the risks associated with these programs before you sign up:

> 1. These programs often require that you deposit money in a special savings account for 36 months or more before all your debts will be settled. Many people have trouble making these payments long enough to get all (or even some) of their debts settled. They drop out the programs

---

17 "About the FTC." Federal Trade Commission. Accessed November 24, 2019. https://www.ftc.gov/about-ftc.

as a result. Before you sign up for a debt settlement program, review your budget carefully to make sure you are financially capable of setting aside the required monthly amounts for the full length of the program.

2. Your creditors have no obligation to agree to negotiate a settlement of the amount you owe. So there is a chance that your debt settlement company will not be able to settle some of your debts—even if you set aside the monthly amounts the program requires. Debt settlement companies also often try to negotiate smaller debts first, leaving interest and fees on large debts to grow.

3. Because debt settlement programs often ask—or encourage—you to stop sending payments directly to your creditors, they may have a negative impact on your credit report and other consequences. For example, your debts may continue to accrue late fees and penalties that can put you further in the hole. You also may get calls from your creditors or debt collectors requesting repayment. You could even be sued for repayment. In some instances, when creditors win a lawsuit, they have the right to garnish your wages or put a lien on your home.

Beware of Debt Settlement Scams

Some companies offering debt settlement programs may engage in deception and fail to deliver on the promises they make—for example, promises or "guarantees" to settle all your credit card debts for, say, 30 to 60 percent of the amount you owe. Other companies may try to collect their own fees from you before they have settled any of your debts—a practice prohibited under the FTC's Telemarketing Sales Rule (TSR) for companies engaged in telemarketing these services. Some fail to explain the risks associated with their programs: for example, that many (or most) consumers drop out without settling their debts, that consumers' credit reports may suffer, or that debt collectors may continue to call you.

Avoid doing business with any company that promises to settle your debt if the company:

- charges any fees before it settles your debts
- touts a "new government program" to bail out personal credit card debt
- guarantees it can make your unsecured debt go away
- tells you to stop communicating with your creditors, but doesn't explain the serious consequences
- tells you it can stop all debt collection calls and lawsuits
- guarantees that your unsecured debts can be paid off for pennies on the dollar

Researching Debt Settlement Companies

Before you enroll in a debt settlement program, do your homework. You're making a big decision that involves spending a lot of your money—money that could go toward paying down your debt. Check out the company with your state Attorney General and local consumer protection agency. They can tell you if any consumer complaints are on file about the firm you're considering doing business with. Ask your state Attorney General if the company is required to be licensed to work in your state and, if so, whether it is.

Enter the name of the company name with the word "complaints" into a search engine. Read what others have said about the companies you're considering, including news about any lawsuits with state or federal regulators for engaging in deceptive or unfair practices.

Fees

If you do business with a debt settlement company, you may have to put money in a dedicated bank account, which will be administered by an independent third party. The funds are yours and you are entitled to the interest that accrues. The account administrator may charge you a reasonable fee for account maintenance, and is responsible for transferring funds from your account to pay your creditors and the debt settlement company when settlements occur.

A company can charge you only a portion of its full fee for each debt it settles. For example, say you owe money to five creditors. The company successfully negotiates a settlement with one of your creditors. The company can charge you only a portion of its full fee at this time because it still needs to successfully negotiate with four other creditors. Each time the debt settlement company successfully settles a debt with one of your creditors, the company can charge you another portion of its full fee. If the company's fees are based on a percentage of the amount you save through the settlement, it must tell you both the percentage it charges and the estimated dollar amount it represents. This may be called a "contingency" fee.

Disclosure Requirements

Before you sign up for the service, the debt relief company must give you information about the program:

- The price and terms: The company must explain its fees and any conditions on its services.

- Results: The company must tell you how long it will take to get results—how many months or years before it will make an offer to each creditor for a settlement.
- Offers: The company must tell you how much money or the percentage of each outstanding debt you must save before it will make an offer to each creditor on your behalf.
- Non-payment: If the company asks you to stop making payments to your creditors—or if the program relies on you to not make payments—it must tell you about the possible negative consequences of your action, including damage to your credit report and credit score; that your creditors may sue you or continue with the collections process; and that your credit card companies may charge you additional fees and interest, which will increase the amount you owe.

The debt relief company also must tell you that:

- the funds are yours and you are entitled to the interest earned;
- the account administrator is not affiliated with the debt relief provider and doesn't get referral fees; and
- you may withdraw your money any time without penalty.

Tax Consequences

Depending on your financial condition, any savings you get from debt relief services can be considered income and taxable. Credit card companies and others may report settled debt to the IRS, which the IRS considers income, unless you are "insolvent." Insolvency is when your total debts are more than the fair market value of your total assets. Insolvency can be complex to determine. Talk to a tax professional if you are not sure whether you qualify for this exception.

Source: United States Federal Trade Commission, ftc.gov[18]

18 "Settling Credit Card Debt." Federal Trade Commission. Accessed November 24, 2019. https://www.consumer.ftc.gov/articles/0145-settling-credit-card-debt.

KNOW YOUR RIGHTS AND STOP DEBT COLLECTOR ABUSE

ARE DEBT COLLECTORS harassing you? There have definitely been some serious cases of debt collector abuse: calling day and night, making threats like jail time, using profanity and telling others (friends, neighbors and family) about your debt.

In fact, the FTC receives more consumer complaints on debt collectors than in any other area.

For some debt collectors the only goal is to muscle money out of you by any means necessary. But they can only get away with unlawful tactics when you don't know your rights. The more you know about what debt collectors can and can't do, the better.

With you in mind, the FTC has outlined your consumer rights as they relate to debt collectors. "The FTC enforces the Fair Debt Collection Practices Act (FDCPA), which makes it illegal for debt collectors to use abusive, unfair, or deceptive practices when they collect debts."[19]

---

19 "Fair Debt Collection Practices Act." Federal Trade Commission. Accessed November 24, 2019. https://www.ftc.gov/system/files/documents/plain-language/fair-debt-collection-practices-act.pdf.

Here are some of the FTC's answers to Debt Collection FAQs:

What types of debts are covered?

Your credit card debt, auto loans, medical bills, student loans, mortgage, and other household debts are covered. Business debts are not.

Can debt collectors contact me any time or any place?

No. Debt collectors can't contact you at inconvenient times or places. They can't contact you before 8 a.m. or after 9 p.m., unless you agree to it. They also can't contact you at work if they're told you're not allowed to get calls there.

How can a debt collector contact me?

Debt collectors can call you, or send letters, emails, or text messages to collect a debt.

How can I stop a debt collector from contacting me?

Send a letter by mail asking for contact to stop (make *yourself* a copy before you do). You might want to send it by certified mail and pay for a "return receipt" so you have a record the collector received it. Once the collector gets your letter, it can only contact you to confirm it will stop contacting you, or to tell you a specific action, like filing a lawsuit, will be taken. If you are represented by an attorney, and inform the collector, the collector must communicate with your attorney, not you, unless the attorney fails to respond within a reasonable period of time to the communication from the debt collector.

You might want to talk to the collector at least once, even if you don't think you owe the debt or can't repay it immediately. That way you can confirm whether it's really your debt. If it is your debt, you can find out from the collector more information about it. In talking with a debt collector, be careful about sharing your personal or financial information, especially if you're not already familiar with the collector.

Can a debt collector contact anyone else about my debt?

A debt collector generally can't discuss your debt with anyone but you or your spouse. If an attorney is representing you, the debt collector has to contact the attorney. A collector can contact other people to find out your address, your home phone number, and where you work, but usually can't contact them more than once.

What does the debt collector have to tell me about the debt?

A collector has to send you a written "validation notice" within five days of first contacting you. The notice has to say:

- how much money you owe
- the name of the creditor you owe it to
- what to do if you don't think it's your debt

What if I don't think I owe the debt?

You can send a debt collector a letter saying you don't owe any or all of the money, or asking for verification of the debt. If you send the letter within 30 days of getting the validation notice, the collector has to send you written verification of the debt, like a copy of a bill for the amount you owe, before it can start trying to collect the debt again. You also can get a collector to stop contacting you, at any time, by sending a letter by mail asking for contact to stop.

What are debt collectors not allowed to do?

They can't harass you. For example, they can't:

- threaten you with violence or harm
- use obscene or profane language
- repeatedly use the phone to annoy you

They can't lie. For example, they can't:

- misrepresent the amount you owe
- lie about being attorneys or government represen-
  tatives
- falsely claim you'll be arrested, or claim legal action will
  be taken against you if it's not true

They can't engage in unfair practices. For example, they can't:

- try to collect interest, fees, or other charges on top of
  the amount you owe, unless the original contract or
  your state law allows it
- deposit a post-dated check early
- take or threaten to take your property unless it can be
  done legally

What should I do if a debt collector sues me?

If a debt collector files a lawsuit against you to collect a
debt, respond to the lawsuit, either personally or through
your lawyer, by the date specified in the court papers to
preserve your rights.

Can a debt collector take money from my paycheck?

Yes, but the collector must first sue you to get a court
order—called a garnishment—that says it can take money
from your paycheck to pay your debts. A collector also can

seek a court order to take money from your bank account. Don't ignore a lawsuit, or you could lose the opportunity to fight a court order.

Source: United States Federal Trade Commission, ftc.gov[20]

For the latest information regarding your consumer rights as it relates to debt collection practices, please visit ftc.gov. To see sample letters used to stop debt collector calls, check out consumerfinance.gov.

ARE YOU BEING SUED FOR YOUR DEBT?

First thing first, do not ignore the lawsuit. It's worth repeating—do not ignore the lawsuit. Review the details and prepare to respond in person or with a lawyer. Per the FTC, responding to the lawsuit by the specified date in court papers preserves your rights.

Here are some additional tips if you're being sued for debt collection:

1. **Verify the debt is actually yours.** This one may sound easy, but I've heard of people paying it just because they were told that they owed it.
2. **Challenge any inaccurate information.** This includes your account balance, interest rate, and any additional fees.

---

20 "Debt Collection FAQs." Federal Trade Commission. Accessed November 24, 2019. https://www.consumer.ftc.gov/articles/debt-collection-faqs.

3. **Appearing in court or having legal representation gives you a voice in the matter.** According to the FTC, "courts frequently granting default judgments against consumers who do not appear or defend themselves."

HAS A DEBT COLLECTOR VIOLATED YOUR RIGHTS?

If a debt collector has violated your consumer rights:

- Report it to your State Attorney General's Office
- File a complaint with the FTC and/or Consumer Financial Protection Bureau
- You have the right to sue the debt collector for violating debt collector laws in pursuing you

WHO IS RESPONSIBLE FOR A LOVED ONE'S DEBT AFTER DEATH?

HAVE YOU EVER wondered what happens to someone's debt after he or she dies? This is hardly a topic anyone wants to think about after losing a loved one. And it's certainly not the kind of conversation people want to have about a loved one's personal affairs, especially when it does not concern them.

Despite this, some debt collectors can do the unthinkable to get paid when people are in a vulnerable state. So here's some guidance from the FTC on debts and deceased relatives:

After a relative dies, the last thing grieving family members want are calls from debt collectors asking them to pay a loved one's debts. As a rule, those debts are paid from the deceased person's estate.

According to the Federal Trade Commission (FTC), the nation's consumer protection agency, family members typically are not obligated to pay the debts of a deceased relative from their own assets. What's more, family members—and all consumers—are protected by the federal Fair Debt Collection Practices Act (FDCPA), which prohibits debt collectors from using abusive, unfair, or deceptive practices to try to collect a debt.

Does a debt go away when the debtor dies?

No. The estate of the deceased person owes the debt. If there isn't enough money in the estate to cover the debt, it typically goes unpaid. But there are exceptions to this rule. You may be responsible for the debt if you:

- co-signed the obligation;
- live in a community property state, such as California;
- are the deceased person's spouse and state law requires you to pay a particular type of debt, like some health care expenses; or
- were legally responsible for resolving the estate and didn't comply with certain state probate laws.

If you have questions about whether you are legally obligated to pay a deceased person's debts from your own assets, talk to a lawyer.

Who has the authority to pay the deceased person's debt out of his or her assets?

The person named in a will who is responsible for settling a deceased person's affairs is called the executor. If there is no will, the court may appoint an administrator, personal representative, or universal successor, and give them the authority to settle the affairs. In some states, others (or other people) may have that authority, even if they haven't been formally appointed by the court.

Whom may a debt collector talk to about a deceased person's debt?

Under the FDCPA, collectors can contact and discuss the deceased person's debts with that person's spouse, parent(s) (if the deceased was a minor child), guardian, executor, or administrator. Also, the FTC permits collectors to contact any other person authorized to pay debts with assets from the deceased person's estate. Debt collectors may not discuss the debts of deceased persons with anyone else.

For Complaints and More Information

Report any problems you have with a debt collector to your state Attorney General's office at naag.org and the Federal Trade Commission at ftccomplaintassistant.gov. Many states have their own debt collection laws that are different from the federal FDCPA. Your Attorney General's office can help you determine your rights under your state's law.

Source: United States Federal Trade Commission, ftc.gov[21]

---

21 "Debts and Deceased Relatives." Federal Trade Commission. Accessed November 24, 2019. https://www.consumer.ftc.gov/ articles/0081-debts-and-deceased-relatives.